CHARLES

Understand Your Emotions and Achieve Inner Peace

Cognitive
BEHAVIORAL
THERAPY

32 STRATEGIES TO MASTER YOUR MIND

The Beginners' At-Home Workbook to Transform Negative Thoughts and Stop Overthinking

© **Copyright 2024 - All rights reserved.**

The content contained within this book may not be reproduced, duplicated, or transmitted without direct written permission from the author or the publisher.

Under no circumstances will any blame or legal responsibility be held against the publisher or author for any damages, reparation, or monetary loss due to the information contained within this book, either directly or indirectly.

Legal Notice:

This book is copyright-protected. It is only for personal use. You cannot amend, distribute, sell, use, quote, or paraphrase any part of this book's content without the author's or publisher's consent.

Disclaimer Notice:

Please note that the information contained within this document is for educational and entertainment purposes only. All effort has been executed to present accurate, up-to-date, reliable, and complete information. No warranties of any kind are declared or implied. Readers acknowledge that the author is not engaged in rendering legal, financial, medical, or professional advice. The content within this book has been derived from various sources. Please consult a licensed professional before attempting any techniques outlined in this book.

By reading this document, the reader agrees that under no circumstances is the author responsible for any direct or indirect losses incurred because of the use of the information contained within this document, including, but not limited to, errors, omissions, or inaccuracies.

Table of Contents

Introduction 7

Chapter 1: Understanding CBT 9
    Why CBT? 10
    Who Will Benefit Most From CBT? 12
    Basic Principles and Foundational Pillars of CBT 14
    How CBT Differs from Other Therapeutic Approaches 17
    FAQ: Cognitive Behavioral Therapy (CBT) 18

Chapter 2: Managing Depression with CBT 23
    Understanding the Symptoms and
    Causes of Depression 24
    Three Approaches to Treating Depression 28
    Building Positive Coping Strategies 44

Chapter 3: Overcoming Anxiety with CBT 47
    Understanding Anxiety Disorders 48
    Three Effective CBT Methods to Control Anxiety 50
    Developing Effective Coping Mechanisms for Anxiety 69

Chapter 4: Curing OCD with CBT 71
    Understanding Obsessive-
    Compulsive Disorder (OCD) 72
    Three Major Approaches for Treating OCD 74
    Create a Structured Plan for Overcoming OCD 83

Chapter 5: Treating Addiction with CBT 85
    Cognitive Interventions for Addiction 88
    Three CBT Strategies for Addiction Intervention 91

Building a Relapse Prevention Plan 100
Personalized Relapse Prevention Plan Worksheet 101

Chapter 6: Managing Insomnia with CBT 105
Understanding the Causes and Impact of Insomnia.........105
Seven Key CBT Components for Managing Insomnia 109
1. Sleep Education..110
2. Cognitive Restructuring for Sleep-related Thoughts 111
3. Sleep Hygiene to Establish Healthy Routines 114
4. Relaxation and Mindfulness Techniques for
Better Sleep 117
5. Establishing a Bed-Sleep Association for
Better Sleep Quality 119
6. Enhancing Sleep Efficiency through
Sleep Restriction...122
7. Sustaining Healthy Sleep Patterns with
Maintenance Strategies..125

Chapter 7: Ways to Cope with Stress Using CBT 129
Understanding the Nature of Stress 130
Identifying Stress Triggers in CBT 132
Challenging Stress-inducing Thoughts................................134
Relaxation Techniques to Reduce Stress..............................138
Thought-Stopping Technique for Stress Management......140
Behavioral Activation for Stress 142

Chapter 8: Overcoming Procrastination with CBT 145
Understanding the Underlying
Causes of Procrastination 146
Cognitive Restructuring to
Overcome Procrastination 147

Behavioral Techniques to Increase
Motivation and Productivity 149
Time-management Strategies for
Overcoming Procrastination 151

Chapter 9: Conquering Negative Emotions with CBT 159
Addressing Negative Emotions 159
Self-compassion 161
Challenging Your Thoughts and Beliefs 169
Practice Gratitude 171
Reframing 173

Conclusion 177

References 183

Exclusive Bonuses 187

Introduction

Today, some are tired of feeling like a prisoner to their own thoughts. Today, someone is stuck in a never-ending cycle of negative emotions, unable to break free. It is sad to think that many do not receive the help they need today; that only prolongs their agony.

But let's be real for a moment. The decision to seek help is not an easy one. It takes courage to acknowledge that something isn't quite right, that you're not living your best life. If this is you, it's okay to feel scared, hesitant, or even skeptical.

It is also okay to make tiny hesitant steps before you leap. Nevertheless, there is no denying that today is a step forward for you. I am aware that you are looking for sensible answers and a few cautious steps to help you find mental freedom. This book provides you with information about Cognitive Behavioral Therapy's (CBT) life-changing potential.

This book is here to guide you through this journey of unlocking doors in your mind that are jarred shut. You will finally understand what's holding you back the entire time.

Everyone deserves to live a beautiful life free from the shackles of mental distress. The transformative power of CBT is worth sharing with everyone. With this book, I hope to reach more people who need help but are afraid to ask anyone for it.

What can you expect from CBT? Imagine finally being able to identify the root causes of your negative thoughts and behaviors and then rewiring your brain to create new, positive patterns. Picture yourself gaining control over your emotions rather than being controlled by them. CBT empowers you to break free from old habits and thought patterns, allowing you to live a life that is authentically yours.

The goal here is not a temporary solution but sustainable change in confronting and resolving deep-seated issues. Cognitive Behavioral Therapy (CBT) is designed for this purpose; it encourages examining and restructuring beliefs and forming new thought patterns. It aims to provide the skills necessary for managing life's challenges with resilience and adaptability.

If you're ready to start your self-help journey, let's explore how CBT can be used to unlock its full potential and open the door to a happier, more fulfilling life.

Chapter 1
Understanding CBT

In today's fast-paced and stressful world, mental health awareness and self-care are essential. Remember, mental health is just as important as physical health, and taking care of it should be a top priority.

One effective approach to managing and nurturing your emotional well-being is through Cognitive Behavioral Therapy (CBT).

In this chapter, you'll gain a comprehensive understanding of Cognitive Behavioral Therapy (CBT) and its transformative potential for your emotional well-being and personal growth.

CBT is a therapeutic technique that focuses on the connection between thoughts, feelings, and behaviors. It aims to help individuals identify and challenge negative thought patterns, replace them with healthier ones, and ultimately improve their emotional well-being.

CBT provides practical strategies that you can implement in your daily life to promote lasting change and achieve emotional freedom and inner peace. CBT techniques have been proven to be highly effective in managing various mental health conditions.

Don't let common misconceptions about CBT cloud your understanding of its effectiveness and potential benefits. Many myths about CBT can prevent individuals from seeking the help they need.

Debunking these misconceptions and understanding the true value of therapy is necessary. One common misconception is that CBT is only for people with severe mental illnesses. In reality, CBT can be beneficial for a wide range of issues, from managing stress and anxiety to improving relationships and self-esteem.

CBT is also often misunderstood as a quick fix or a one-size-fits-all solution. However, it's a collaborative process that requires active participation and commitment.

Why CBT?

Cognitive Behavioral Therapy (CBT) is a widely recognized and effective form of therapy that can benefit individuals in various ways. Here are some reasons why one should be interested in CBT:

- **Evidence-based:** CBT is supported by extensive scientific research and has been proven to be effective in treating a wide range of mental health conditions, including anxiety disorders, depression, phobias, and eating disorders.

- **Practical approach:** CBT focuses on the present and provides practical tools and strategies to help individuals identify and change unhelpful thoughts and behaviors. It emphasizes problem-solving and equips individuals with skills they can use in their daily lives.

- **Empowerment:** CBT empowers individuals to take an active role in their own therapy. It helps them develop self-awareness and a deeper understanding of their thoughts and emotions, enabling them to become more self-reliant in managing their mental health.

- **Long-lasting results:** CBT aims to bring about lasting changes by targeting the underlying patterns of thinking and behavior that contribute to distress. It equips individuals with skills they can continue to use even after therapy ends, allowing them to maintain their progress in the long term.

Apart from CBT with a therapist, reading this book can offer readers several benefits:

- A CBT book can provide individuals with a self-guided approach to understanding and applying CBT techniques. It offers practical exercises, worksheets, and case examples that readers can work through at their own pace.

- It is generally more affordable than therapy sessions, making them a more accessible option for individuals who may not have the means or desire to engage in therapy.

- Even if someone is already undergoing CBT with a therapist, reading CBT books can serve as a supplemental resource. It can reinforce the concepts and techniques learned in therapy and provide additional insights and strategies.

Who Will Benefit Most From CBT?

CBT is suitable for a wide range of individuals, including:

Those with mental health conditions	CBT has been proven effective in treating various mental health conditions such as anxiety disorders, depression, post-traumatic stress disorder (PTSD), obsessive-compulsive disorder (OCD), and more.
Individuals seeking personal growth	CBT can also benefit individuals who are not necessarily experiencing a diagnosed mental health condition but are looking to enhance their overall well-being, improve their coping skills, and develop healthier thinking patterns.
Those open to self-reflection and change	CBT requires individuals to be open to examining their thoughts, beliefs, and behaviors. It is most effective when individuals are willing to challenge and modify unhelpful patterns.

While CBT can be highly effective, it may not be suitable for everyone. It is always recommended to consult with a mental health professional to determine the most appropriate treatment approach for an individual's specific needs.

Before committing oneself to CBT, there are a few questions to ask yourself:

- **Are you willing to actively participate?**
  CBT requires active participation and engagement from the individual. It involves challenging and changing unhelpful thoughts and behaviors, which can sometimes be uncomfortable or challenging.

- **Are you willing to commit to this task?**
  CBT is not an overnight solution. It requires time and effort to practice and apply the techniques learned in therapy consistently. Consistency and commitment are key to achieving positive results.

The success of any program, including Cognitive Behavioral Therapy (CBT), depends on your dedication to making life-altering changes and your sincere intentions.

So, *why should you read on to discover more about CBT?* If you're looking for a practical and successful way to improve your mental health, learning more about CBT is well worth your time. CBT may help you generate good and sustainable change in your life by arming you with practical tools, conquering common mental health difficulties, and improving your overall well-being. Continue reading to learn more about CBT and how it may help you live a happier and healthier life.

Basic Principles and Foundational Pillars of CBT

If this is your first time delving deeper into the principles of CBT, or if you are going through or wish to engage in therapy, it is critical to grasp the basics. To further understand how CBT works, let's start with cognition levels.

---

3 Levels of Cognition

Core Beliefs

These are deeply ingrained beliefs that we develop based on our childhood experiences. They shape how we view ourselves, our environment, and the future. By examining and challenging these core beliefs, we can work towards developing more balanced and realistic perspectives.

Dysfunctional Assumptions

Humans tend to hold onto negative thoughts more easily than positive ones. These cognitive distortions are irrational thought patterns that distort our perceptions of reality. Examples include all-or-nothing thinking (viewing things in black and white terms), "should" statements (believing we should never make mistakes), and overgeneralization (thinking that things will never improve). CBT helps individuals recognize and challenge these distortions to promote more positive thinking.

Automatic Negative Thoughts
These are involuntary negative perceptions of reality that occur out of habit. They are often brief and can cause negative emotions. By becoming aware of these automatic negative thoughts, individuals can learn to challenge and replace them with more constructive and realistic thoughts.

The Goal

The goal of CBT is to change how we think about situations and how we respond to them, ultimately leading to a change in our emotions. It is important to note that everyone experiences distorted thoughts at times, but we have the power to choose how we respond to them. With practice, we can learn to challenge these thoughts and develop more compassionate and helpful ways of thinking.

The Role of Thoughts, Emotions, and Behaviors in CBT

Understanding how thoughts, emotions, and behaviors are interconnected is pivotal in Cognitive Behavioral Therapy (CBT), as it allows you to gain insight into the ways your thinking patterns influence your feelings and actions.

Consider the following example:

> **Scenario:** Sarah is a high school student who is anxious about an upcoming math test. She has a history of struggling with math and often worries about failing.

Thoughts: Sarah's thoughts play a crucial role in shaping her emotions and behavior in this scenario. She may have negative and distorted thoughts such as *"I'm terrible at math," "I'll never understand this,"* or *"I'm going to fail this test."* These thoughts are unhelpful and contribute to her feeling anxious and overwhelmed.

Emotions: Sarah's negative thoughts trigger intense emotions, such as fear, anxiety, and frustration. She may feel a sense of dread, experience physical symptoms like a racing heart or sweaty palms, and have difficulty concentrating on studying.

Behaviors: Sarah's emotions and thoughts influence her behaviors. Due to her anxiety, she may avoid studying or procrastinate because she feels overwhelmed and believes she won't be able to succeed. She may also engage in negative self-talk, telling herself there's no point in studying because she will fail anyway.

Interconnectedness: In this scenario, Sarah's thoughts, emotions, and behaviors are interconnected in a cyclical relationship. Her negative thoughts fuel her anxiety and fear, which then impact her behavior by leading to avoidance or procrastination. This, in turn, reinforces her negative thoughts and perpetuates the cycle of anxiety and poor performance.

In CBT, Sarah would work with a therapist to identify and challenge her cognitive distortions. By examining the evidence for and against her negative thoughts, she can develop more balanced and rational thinking patterns. For example, she may reframe her thoughts to *"I may find math challenging, but I have the ability to learn and improve,"* or *"Even if I don't get a perfect score, it doesn't define my worth or future success."*

By replacing her negative thoughts with more realistic and positive ones, Sarah can begin to change her emotions and behavior. She may feel more confident and motivated to study, leading to improved performance and reduced anxiety. Over time, this new cycle of positive thoughts, emotions, and behaviors can become ingrained, promoting emotional well-being and academic success.

This example demonstrates how thoughts, emotions, and behaviors are interconnected in CBT and highlights the importance of identifying and challenging cognitive distortions to promote positive change.

How CBT Differs from Other Therapeutic Approaches

To differentiate Cognitive Behavioral Therapy (CBT) from other therapeutic approaches, it's important to highlight its distinctive focus on modifying negative thought patterns and behaviors to promote emotional well-being.

CBT	Other Therapeutic Approaches
Present-focused, exploring thoughts, emotions, and behaviors in the here and now	Focus on unconscious mind and childhood experiences

Action-oriented and goal-driven, empowering active participation in the healing process	Reliance on introspection and self-reflection
Evidence-based techniques supported by scientific research	Reliance on intuition and subjective interpretations
Consistently shown positive results in alleviating symptoms of various mental health conditions	Varied outcomes depending on the therapeutic approach
Equips individuals with lifelong skills to manage stress and maintain emotional well-being	May not provide long-lasting changes or skills for ongoing self-management

Furthermore, CBT utilizes a wide range of techniques tailored to your specific needs and goals. By employing varied therapeutic methods, CBT can address the unique complexities of your individual experience and provide a personalized approach to your healing journey.

FAQ: Cognitive Behavioral Therapy (CBT)

1. **What conditions can CBT treat?**
   CBT has been found to be effective in treating a wide range of mental health conditions, including anxiety disorders (such as generalized anxiety disorder, social anxiety disorder, and panic disorder), depression, post-traumatic stress disorder (PTSD),

obsessive-compulsive disorder (OCD), eating disorders, and substance abuse disorders.

2. **How long does CBT treatment typically last?**
The duration of CBT treatment can vary depending on the individual and the specific condition being treated. Generally, CBT is a short-term therapy consisting of about 12 to 20 sessions, but it can be longer or shorter depending on the severity and complexity of the issues being addressed.

3. **Is CBT only about changing thoughts?**
While changing negative thoughts is an important aspect of CBT, it also emphasizes modifying behaviors. CBT encourages individuals to engage in activities that promote positive mental health and well-being and to gradually confront and overcome fears or avoidance behaviors.

4. **Is CBT suitable for everyone?**
CBT can be beneficial for many individuals, but it may not be the most appropriate treatment for everyone. It is important to consult with a qualified mental health professional to determine if CBT is the right approach for your specific needs and circumstances.

5. **Can CBT be effective without medication?**
Yes, CBT can be effective without medication. However, in some cases, a combination of medication and CBT may be recommended, especially for individuals with severe symptoms or certain conditions. It is best to discuss your options with a healthcare provider.

6. **How long does it take to see results from CBT?**
   The timeline for seeing results from CBT can vary depending on the individual and the severity of the condition being treated. Some individuals may start experiencing improvements within a few weeks, while others may require several months of consistent therapy to see significant changes.

7. **Can CBT be done online or through self-help resources?**
   Yes, CBT can be delivered through online platforms or self-help resources, such as books, apps, or online therapy sessions. However, it is important to ensure that the resources are evidence-based and provided by qualified professionals. For more complex or severe conditions, working with a trained therapist in person or online is often recommended.

8. **Will CBT cure my mental health condition?**
   CBT is not a cure for mental health conditions, but it can provide individuals with effective tools and strategies to manage their symptoms and improve their overall well-being. It equips individuals with lifelong skills to navigate challenges and maintain good mental health.

Remember, these FAQ answers are intended for informational purposes only and should not replace professional advice. For personalized guidance and treatment, it is important to consult with a qualified mental health professional.

Understanding the fundamentals of CBT will offer you greater confidence and clarity as you use it to alter your life, one thought, emotion, and behavior at a time. Rather than mindlessly following a program, it is better to be an informed participant in a collaborative effort with your therapist to live your highest potential. Although knowledge and proven methods are vital in CBT, you ultimately determine your own success.

Chapter 2
Managing Depression with CBT

Depression is a mental health disorder characterized by persistent feelings of sadness, hopelessness, and a lack of interest or pleasure in activities. If you are experiencing this, you are not alone, and help is available.

Depression affects millions of people worldwide and can have a significant impact on their daily lives, relationships, and overall well-being. While there are various treatment options available, one effective approach is Cognitive Behavioral Therapy (CBT).

CBT is typically conducted in a structured and time-limited manner, often consisting of 12-20 sessions. The therapist and client work collaboratively to set specific goals and develop strategies to address the client's unique challenges. Throughout the therapy process, individuals learn to recognize and challenge negative thoughts and beliefs that contribute to their depressive symptoms. This chapter will explain how this is done.

This chapter also discusses behavioral activation, which involves engaging in pleasurable and meaningful activities to counteract the lack of interest and pleasure associated with depression. By gradually increasing the individual's activity level and involvement in positive experiences, CBT helps to improve mood and motivation.

You will also learn to incorporate cognitive restructuring, which involves identifying and changing irrational or unhelpful thoughts and beliefs. By challenging negative thinking patterns and replacing them with more realistic and positive thoughts, individuals can develop a more balanced and adaptive perspective.

Overall, Cognitive Behavioral Therapy offers a practical and evidence-based approach to treating depression. Take the first step to understanding depression better and develop healthier thinking patterns and behaviors, leading to improved mood and functioning.

Understanding the Symptoms and Causes of Depression

Understand the symptoms and causes of depression to gain insight into your emotional well-being and take steps towards managing it effectively. Depression is a complex and often misunderstood mental health condition. It's important to recognize the symptoms and understand the underlying causes in order to seek appropriate treatment and support.

Symptoms of depression can vary from person to person. It's crucial to pay attention to these signs and seek help if you or someone you know is experiencing them.

- **Persistent sadness or a low mood**: Feeling down or experiencing a deep sadness that lasts for most of the day, nearly every day.
- **Loss of interest or pleasure in activities**: Losing interest or enjoyment in activities that were once enjoyable, such as hobbies, socializing, or even sex.
- **Significant weight loss or gain**: A noticeable change in appetite that results in significant weight loss or gain without intentional dieting.
- **Insomnia or excessive sleeping**: Trouble falling asleep, staying asleep, or experiencing excessive sleepiness, which can lead to changes in sleep patterns.
- **Restlessness or slowed movements**: Feeling restless, agitated, or having difficulty sitting still, or on the contrary, experiencing slowed movements and a noticeable decrease in physical activity.
- **Fatigue or loss of energy**: Feeling constantly tired, lacking energy, and finding it difficult to perform everyday tasks or even small activities.
- **Feelings of worthlessness or excessive guilt**: Experiencing persistent feelings of guilt, worthlessness, or self-blame, even when there is no logical reason for these emotions.
- **Difficulty concentrating or making decisions**: Having trouble focusing, making decisions, or experiencing a significant decline in cognitive abilities, such as memory and problem-solving skills.
- **Recurrent thoughts of death or suicide**: Having frequent thoughts about death, dying, or suicidal ideation. This can range from fleeting thoughts to detailed planning.

- **Physical symptoms**: Experiencing unexplained physical symptoms such as headaches, digestive issues, or chronic pain, which do not respond to medical treatment.
- **Social withdrawal or isolation**: Withdrawing from social activities, avoiding friends or family, and preferring to be alone rather than engaging in social interactions.
- **Irritability or mood swings**: Feeling easily irritated, agitated, or having frequent mood swings, which can lead to strained relationships with others.

Experiencing a few of these symptoms occasionally is normal, but if they persist for a prolonged period (at least two weeks) and significantly interfere with daily functioning, it may indicate clinical depression. If you or someone you know is experiencing these symptoms, it is recommended to seek professional help.

The causes of depression, on the other hand, can be multifaceted and differ from individual to individual. Here are the ten common causes of depression.

1. **Genetics:** Family history of depression or mental illnesses
2. **Brain Chemistry Imbalance:** Disruption in neurotransmitters like serotonin, norepinephrine, and dopamine. Such may lead to difficulty concentrating, changes in appetite, and sleep disturbances.
3. **Hormonal Changes:** Fluctuations in estrogen and progesterone levels which can manifest as mood swings, irritability, fatigue, changes in appetite.
4. **Chronic Illness:** Dealing with long-term health conditions like cancer, diabetes, or chronic pain.

5. **Traumatic Life Events:** Experiencing abuse, loss of a loved one, or a major life change.
6. **Substance Abuse:** Regular use of drugs or alcohol
7. **Social Isolation:** Lack of social support or feeling disconnected from others
8. **Chronic Stress:** Long-term exposure to high levels of stress, such as work pressure or financial problems
9. **Personality Traits:** Certain personality traits, like perfectionism or pessimism, can contribute to depression
10. **Medications:** Side effects of certain medications, such as some antidepressants or hormonal contraceptives

Understanding the causes and symptoms of depression is essential for developing an effective treatment plan. The severity and complexity of depression's causes and symptoms can vary, as can the ways in which different people experience and react to them. These elements are part of the downward spiral that should be taken as key information to look into. It is crucial to begin cognitive-behavioral therapy (CBT) by determining the origins and factors that cause distress. You will then be able to take the required actions to effect change as swiftly as possible.

For a more precise diagnosis, working with a therapist and consulting a specialist is recommended. But having self-awareness will make you more prepared, particularly under trying circumstances. You will be able to see the emotional and behavioral patterns that are specific to you and that result from depression.

Three Approaches to Treating Depression

If you're struggling with depression, cognitive behavioral therapy (CBT) offers highly effective and practical approaches to help you rewire your mind and find emotional freedom. CBT techniques focus on changing negative thought patterns and behaviors that contribute to depression, allowing you to regain control over your life and find lasting relief.

1. Identifying Negative Thinking Patterns

Identifying negative thinking patterns in Cognitive Behavioral Therapy (CBT) helps with depression by uncovering and challenging distorted thoughts and beliefs that contribute to depressive symptoms. Negative thinking patterns, also known as cognitive distortions, are thought patterns that are biased and irrational, leading to negative emotions and behaviors.

By identifying these patterns, individuals can become more aware of the negative thoughts that influence their mood and behavior. This process involves recognizing common cognitive distortions, such as all-or-nothing thinking, overgeneralization, mental filtering, and personalization.

Once these negative thinking patterns are identified, CBT helps individuals challenge and reframe these thoughts by providing evidence-based techniques. This may involve examining the accuracy and validity of the negative thoughts, finding alternative explanations or interpretations, and considering more balanced and realistic perspectives. By doing so, individuals can gradually replace negative thoughts with more positive and adaptive ones.

By following these steps, you can begin to change your mindset and break free from the grip of negativity.

Step 1: Awareness
Start by becoming aware of your thoughts throughout the day. Notice when negative thoughts arise and the situations or triggers that tend to bring them up. For example, you may notice that when you make a mistake at work, you immediately think, *"I'm such a failure."*

Step 2: Identify Cognitive Distortions
Once you've become aware of your negative thoughts, it's time to identify the cognitive distortions that may be at play. Cognitive distortions are irrational and negative thought patterns that can distort your perception of reality. Some common distortions include:

Cognitive Distortions

All-or-nothing thinking	Seeing things as black or white, with no shades of gray. For example, thinking, *"If I'm not perfect, then I'm a complete failure."*
Overgeneralization	Making broad conclusions based on a single event. For example, thinking, *"I made a mistake in this presentation, so I'll never be successful."*

Personalization	Taking responsibility for things that are beyond your control. For example, thinking, *"My friend canceled our plans because they don't like me."*
Catastrophizing	Exaggerating the negative outcomes of a situation and expecting the worst possible outcome. For example, thinking, *'If I fail this test, my life will be ruined and I'll never amount to anything.'*
Mental filtering	Focusing only on the negative aspects of a situation and ignoring any positive aspects. For example, discounting compliments and only remembering criticism.
Emotional reasoning	Believing that your emotions reflect reality. For example, thinking, *'I feel like a failure, so I must be a failure.'*
Jumping to conclusions	Making assumptions without sufficient evidence. This can include mind-reading, where you assume you know what others are thinking, or fortune-telling, where you predict negative outcomes without any evidence to support it.

Should statements	Putting excessive pressure on yourself by using words like *'should,'* *'must,'* or *'ought to.'* For example, thinking, *'I should have accomplished more by this age.'*
Discounting the positive	Minimizing or dismissing positive experiences or achievements. For example, thinking, *'This success was just luck, it doesn't really count.'*
Labeling	Attaching negative labels to yourself or others based on a single characteristic or mistake. For example, thinking, *'I'm such a failure'* or *'They're a terrible person.'*

Recognize these cognitive distortions and challenge them with more realistic and balanced thoughts. This can help reduce the negative impact they have on your mood and overall well-being.

Step 3: Challenge Negative Thoughts
Once you've identified the cognitive distortions, it's time to challenge and replace them with more realistic and positive thoughts. Ask yourself these questions:

1. **Is there evidence to support this negative thought?**
   Look for evidence that supports or contradicts your negative thoughts. For example, if you think, *"I'm a failure,"* ask yourself, *"Have I ever succeeded in anything before?"*

2. **What are alternative explanations or viewpoints?**
   Consider alternative explanations or viewpoints that are more balanced and realistic. For example, instead of thinking, *"I'll never be successful,"* consider thinking, *"Everyone makes mistakes, and I can learn from this experience."*

3. **What advice would I give to a friend in this situation?**
   Imagine a friend going through a similar situation. What advice would you give them? Apply that advice to yourself.

Step 4: Practice Self-Compassion

Be compassionate and gentle with yourself throughout this process. Changing negative thought patterns takes time and effort. Treat yourself with kindness and understanding, just as you would a close friend. Remind yourself that it's okay to make mistakes and that you're actively working on improving your mindset.

Step 5: Repeat and Reinforce

Negative thought patterns can be deeply ingrained, so it's important to repeat these steps consistently. Challenge and replace negative thoughts whenever they arise, and reinforce positive and realistic thinking. Over time, this practice will help rewire your brain and create new, healthier thought patterns.

When you find it difficult to challenge negative thoughts on your own, consider seeking support from a mental health professional who can guide you through the process.

The power to change your mindset and break free from negative thought patterns is within you. With practice and perseverance, you can cultivate a more positive and empowering outlook on life.

2. Positive Affirmations, Self-compassion, and Mindfulness

Because they are simple and convenient to perform on your own, these three self-help techniques are likely among the most tried-and-true and well-liked ones. But how might they be most effective on the dark path of depression?

Here you can incorporate them along with challenging and reframing negative thoughts by actively confronting the cognitive distortions identified previously and replacing them with something that promotes a healthier mindset.

By incorporating positive affirmations, self-compassion, and mindfulness exercises into your daily routine, you can rewire your mind to focus on the positive aspects of yourself and your life. This guide aims to provide you with actionable strategies to challenge negative thoughts, cultivate self-compassion, and develop a more balanced perspective.

Step 1: Recognize Cognitive Distortions
Before challenging cognitive distortions, it's important to recognize them. Cognitive distortions are irrational thoughts or beliefs that can negatively impact our emotions and behaviors. Take a moment to reflect on your thoughts and identify any recurring patterns of negative thinking.

Step 2: Create a List of Positive Affirmations

Positive affirmations are powerful statements that counteract negative thoughts and beliefs. Start by creating a list of affirmations that resonate with you. These affirmations should focus on your strengths, capabilities, and self-worth. For example:

> *"I am capable of overcoming challenges."*
> *"I am worthy of love and happiness."*
> *"I am deserving of success."*

Step 3: Repeat Affirmations Daily

Choose a few affirmations from your list and repeat them daily, preferably in front of a mirror. Say them with conviction and believe in their truth. Repetition is key to rewiring your mind and replacing negative thoughts with positive ones. Incorporate affirmations into your morning or bedtime routine to set a positive tone for the day or promote restful sleep.

Step 4: Practice Self-Compassion

Self-compassion involves treating yourself with kindness and understanding. When negative thoughts arise, practice self-compassion by offering yourself words of comfort and support. Remind yourself that everyone makes mistakes and that it's okay to not be perfect. For example:

> *"I am human, and it's natural to have flaws."*
> *"I deserve kindness and understanding, just like anyone else."*

Step 5: Replace Negative Thoughts with Compassionate Ones
Whenever you catch yourself engaging in negative self-talk, consciously replace those thoughts with compassionate and understanding ones. Imagine what you would say to a dear friend in a similar situation and offer yourself the same level of kindness. This practice will help challenge negative thoughts and foster self-compassion.

Step 6: Cultivate Mindfulness
Incorporate mindfulness exercises into your daily routine to cultivate awareness and detachment from negative thoughts. Set aside a few minutes each day to practice mindfulness. Focus on your breath or engage in a body scan exercise, observing any thoughts or sensations without judgment. This practice will help you gain a better understanding of negative thoughts' origins and challenge their validity.

Step 7: Reframe Negative Thoughts
Using the insights gained from mindfulness, actively reframe negative thoughts into more balanced and realistic perspectives. Ask yourself questions like:

"Is there evidence to support this thought?"
"Am I focusing only on the negatives and ignoring the positives?"
"What would a more rational and compassionate perspective be?"

Remember to be patient and kind to yourself throughout this process. You deserve happiness, love, and self-acceptance. Simple as these exercises may be, making them a regular part of your routine might help illuminate the shadowy areas where your sadness lurks.

3. Behavioral Activation Techniques

Behavioral activation (BA) is a key component of Cognitive Behavioral Therapy (CBT) used to address depression. It is based on the idea that depression is maintained by a lack of engagement in reinforcing activities, which leads to a decrease in positive emotions and an increase in negative thoughts and feelings. BA aims to increase the frequency of rewarding activities and improve mood by targeting behavior patterns.

How Behavioral Activation Works to Address Depression

Activity monitoring Identifying and monitoring an individual's daily activities, including those that provide a sense of pleasure, accomplishment, or mastery. This helps to identify patterns of behavior and determine which activities may be contributing to or maintaining depression.
Activity scheduling Scheduling specific activities that align with a person's values and goals. You can work together with a therapist to create a daily or weekly schedule that includes a balance of pleasurable and meaningful activities.
Gradual increase in activity level BA focuses on gradually increasing the frequency and duration of activities over time. This helps individuals overcome the inertia and lack of motivation often associated with depression. Starting with small, achievable goals, individuals work towards engaging in more activities that bring them joy and a sense of accomplishment.

Behavioral activation hierarchy
Creating a hierarchy of activities, ranging from the least to the most challenging. This allows the individual to gradually face and engage in activities they may have been avoiding due to depression. By tackling activities in a step-by-step manner, they can build confidence and increase their overall activity level.
Challenging negative thoughts
BA also involves identifying and challenging negative thoughts or beliefs that may be hindering engagement in activities. Individuals will recognize and reframe negative thoughts, replacing them with more positive and realistic ones.
Problem-solving
BA incorporates problem-solving techniques to address barriers and challenges that may arise during activity engagement. Identify potential obstacles and develop strategies to overcome them, promoting a sense of self-efficacy.

Behavioral activation techniques aim to reverse the downward spiral of depression by systematically increasing positive activity and reducing avoidance behaviors. This approach helps individuals regain a sense of pleasure, accomplishment, and connection, leading to improvements in mood and overall well-being.

Apply BA and start bringing about positive changes today by simply following these steps:

Step 1: Activity Monitoring

- Begin by keeping a daily record of your activities, including pleasurable and necessary tasks.

- Use a journal or a digital app to track your activities throughout the day, noting the time spent on each activity and your level of enjoyment or accomplishment.
- This will help you identify patterns and gain insight into which activities contribute to your well-being and which may be maintaining your depression.
- Be honest and thorough in monitoring, paying attention to positive and negative experiences.

> **Example:** If you notice that spending time with loved ones brings you joy and boosts your mood, make a note of it in your activity log. Similarly, if you find that certain tasks drain your energy or make you feel overwhelmed, take note of that as well.

Step 2: Increase Motivation

- Take a few moments to reflect on activities that bring you joy or a sense of accomplishment. These can be simple things like going for a walk, practicing a hobby, or spending quality time with loved ones.
- Make a list of these activities and choose one to start with. It's important to select something achievable and realistic for you.
- Set aside dedicated time each day or week for this activity. Treat it as a non-negotiable appointment with yourself.
- Notice how engaging in this activity makes you feel. Pay attention to any increase in motivation, happiness, or sense of purpose.

> **Example:** Let's say you enjoy painting. Allocate 30 minutes each day to sit down with your art supplies and create something. Treat it as a special time for yourself, where you can express your creativity and immerse yourself in the process. Notice how this activity brings you joy and a renewed sense of motivation.

Step 3: Activity Scheduling

- Collaborate with a therapist or use self-reflection to identify activities that align with your values and goals.
- Create a daily or weekly schedule that includes a balance of pleasurable and meaningful activities.
- Consider factors such as time constraints, energy levels, and personal preferences when scheduling activities.
- Stick to your schedule as much as possible, treating it as a commitment to your well-being.

> **Example:** If you value self-care, schedule activities like taking a warm bath, practicing mindfulness, or engaging in a hobby that brings you joy. If career growth is important to you, schedule time for professional development or networking opportunities.

Step 4: Set Clear, Achievable Goals

- Identify an area of your life where you would like to make positive changes. This could be related to your career, relationships, health, or personal growth.

- Break down your larger goal into smaller, manageable steps. Each step should be specific, measurable, achievable, relevant, and time-bound (SMART).
- Write down your goals and keep them somewhere visible, like a journal or a vision board. This will serve as a reminder of what you're working towards and keep you focused.
- Celebrate your successes along the way. When you achieve a smaller goal, take a moment to acknowledge and reward yourself. This positive reinforcement will help keep you motivated and committed.

> Example: Let's say your goal is to improve your physical fitness. Break it down into smaller steps such as going for a 30-minute walk three times a week, incorporating strength training exercises twice a week, and gradually increasing the duration and intensity of your workouts. Celebrate each milestone by treating yourself to something you enjoy, like a relaxing bath or a new workout outfit.

Step 5: Reinforce Positive Behaviors

- Identify behaviors that align with your goals and bring you closer to the life you want to create. These can include self-care, healthy boundaries, gratitude, and positive self-talk.
- Commit to engaging in these behaviors regularly. Start by selecting one or two that feel achievable and relevant to you.

- Create reminders or cues to prompt you to engage in these behaviors. For example, you can set alarms on your phone or place sticky notes in visible areas.
- Reflect on the positive impact these behaviors have on your mindset and overall well-being. Notice any changes in your thoughts, emotions, or behaviors as a result of reinforcing positive actions.

Example: Let's say you want to practice gratitude. Commit to writing down three things you're grateful for each day. Set a reminder on your phone to prompt you to pause and reflect on your blessings. Notice how this practice shifts your mindset and helps you appreciate the positive aspects of your life.

Step 6: Gradual Increase in Activity Level

- Start with small, achievable goals to overcome the inertia and lack of motivation associated with depression.
- Gradually increase the frequency and duration of activities over time.
- Challenge yourself to engage in more activities that bring you joy and a sense of accomplishment.
- Celebrate each milestone and acknowledge the progress you make, no matter how small.

> **Example:** If you haven't been exercising regularly, start by going for a short walk three times a week. As you build momentum and confidence, gradually increase the duration and frequency of your walks. Eventually, you may even consider trying new forms of exercise or joining a fitness class.

Step 7: Behavioral Activation Hierarchy

- Create a hierarchy of activities, starting from the least challenging to the most challenging.
- This allows you to gradually face and engage in activities you may have been avoiding due to depression.
- Break down each activity into smaller, manageable steps.
- By tackling activities in a step-by-step manner, you can build confidence and increase your overall activity level.

> **Example:** If socializing has been difficult for you, start by reaching out to a close friend for a virtual hangout. Once you feel comfortable with that, challenge yourself to attend a small gathering or join a social club with shared interests.

Step 8: Challenging Negative Thoughts

- Become aware of any negative thoughts or beliefs that may be hindering your engagement in activities.
- Challenge and reframe these negative thoughts, replacing them with more positive and realistic ones.

- Practice self-compassion and remind yourself that you are capable of change and growth.

> **Example:** If you find yourself thinking, *"I'm not good enough"* when it comes to pursuing a new hobby, challenge that thought by reminding yourself that everyone starts as a beginner and improvement comes with practice and dedication.

Step 9: Problem-Solving

- Anticipate potential obstacles or challenges that may arise during activity engagement.
- Develop strategies to overcome these obstacles, promoting a sense of self-efficacy.
- Seek support from loved ones or professional help if needed.
- Remember that problem-solving is an ongoing process, and it's okay to adjust your approach as you learn and grow.

> **Example:** If lack of time is a barrier to engaging in activities, brainstorm ways to prioritize and carve out dedicated time. This may involve delegating tasks, setting boundaries, or reevaluating your schedule.

By incorporating these additional techniques into your behavioral activation practice, you can further enhance your motivation, goal-setting, and overall well-being.

Remember, these behavioral activation techniques are not a quick fix but rather a process of consistent effort and self-reflection. With time and practice, you will begin to see positive changes in your mindset, happiness, and inner peace.

Building Positive Coping Strategies

Depression is a difficult journey, but remember that you are not alone. Each person's experience with depression is unique, and the coping strategies that work for one person may not work for another. However, there are some steps you can take to create and develop effective coping strategies that can equip you in your battle against depression.

- **Identify your triggers.** Take the time to recognize the situations, thoughts, or emotions that tend to worsen your depressive symptoms. By understanding what sets off these feelings, you can better prepare yourself to navigate through them.

- **Experiment with coping techniques.** Try out different strategies, such as exercise, mindfulness, journaling, or engaging in hobbies that bring you joy. Keep an open mind and give yourself the space to explore what works best for you. Remember, finding effective coping mechanisms may take time, so be patient and gentle with yourself.

- **Monitor your progress.** Track your moods, symptoms, and the effectiveness of different coping strategies. This will help you identify patterns and make adjustments as needed.

Remember that progress may not always be linear, so don't be discouraged if you have setbacks along the way. Use these setbacks as opportunities for growth and learning.

- **Seek professional guidance.** Consider working with a therapist or counselor who specializes in depression. They can provide personalized coping strategies and support tailored to your specific needs. Remember, reaching out for help is a sign of strength, not weakness.

- **Be consistent when it comes to coping with depression.** Implement the coping strategies that work well for you consistently. Building effective coping mechanisms takes time and repetition. Be patient and stay committed to your self-care routine.

Always remember that you are not alone. Reach out to loved ones for support and surround yourself with a strong support system. Remember to be kind to yourself and practice self-compassion.

In times when you feel overwhelmed, remember these wise words from Helen Keller, *"Although the world is full of suffering, it is also full of the overcoming of it."* You have the strength within you to overcome depression and find joy in life again. Keep fighting, keep believing, and never forget that there is always hope.

And finally, let me leave you with this powerful quotation from Rumi: *"The wound is the place where the light enters you."* Embrace your wounds, for they have the potential to transform you and lead you to a place of healing and growth.

Chapter 3
Overcoming Anxiety with CBT

Cognitive Behavioral Therapy (CBT) is an effective approach to treating anxiety due to several key factors.

1. CBT focuses on thoughts and behaviors, acknowledging that anxiety is often fueled by negative thinking patterns and unhelpful actions. By challenging and changing these cognitive distortions and maladaptive behaviors, individuals can experience a reduction in anxiety symptoms.

2. CBT is a collaborative and active therapy involving the individual in setting goals, identifying triggers, and learning coping strategies. This active involvement empowers individuals to take ownership of their anxiety and develop effective strategies to manage it.

3. CBT utilizes evidence-based techniques such as cognitive restructuring, exposure therapy, relaxation techniques, and problem-solving skills. These techniques have been scientifically proven to be effective in treating anxiety. Additionally, CBT is a short-term and time-limited therapy, which allows individuals to focus on specific goals and experience a sense of progress and achievement relatively quickly.

4. CBT also takes a holistic approach by addressing multiple factors that contribute to anxiety, including emotions, physical sensations, and environmental factors. This comprehensive approach helps individuals gain a deeper understanding of their anxiety and develop a wide range of strategies to manage it effectively.

5. Lastly, CBT equips individuals with skills and knowledge to prevent relapse and maintain progress. By identifying early warning signs, developing coping strategies, and building resilience, individuals are better equipped to handle future challenges and prevent the re-emergence of anxiety symptoms.

In this chapter, you'll learn how to overcome anxiety using Cognitive Behavioral Therapy (CBT). Anxiety can be debilitating, making it difficult to enjoy life and engage in daily activities. But with the right tools and techniques, you can regain control over your thoughts and emotions and find relief from anxiety.

Understanding Anxiety Disorders

One of the key components in understanding anxiety disorders is recognizing the impact they can have on your daily life and well-being. Anxiety disorders are more than just occasional worry or nervousness. They can disrupt your relationships, work, and overall quality of life. It's important to understand the causes of anxiety in order to effectively manage and overcome it.

The impact of anxiety on daily life can be far-reaching. It can affect your ability to concentrate, sleep, and perform daily tasks. It can also lead to physical symptoms such as headaches, stomachaches, and muscle tension.

There are several types of anxiety disorders, including generalized anxiety disorder, panic disorder, social anxiety disorder, and specific phobias. Each type has its own unique symptoms and triggers, but they all share the common theme of excessive and irrational fear or worry.

1. **Generalized Anxiety Disorder (GAD)**: This is characterized by excessive worry and anxiety about various aspects of life, such as work, relationships, finances, or health. People with GAD often find it difficult to control their worries and may experience physical symptoms like restlessness, fatigue, muscle tension, and difficulty concentrating. The triggers for GAD can be both specific events or more generalized stressors.

2. **Panic Disorder**: Individuals with panic disorder experience sudden and recurring panic attacks. These attacks are intense periods of fear or discomfort that reach a peak within minutes and include symptoms like rapid heartbeat, sweating, trembling, shortness of breath, and a sense of impending doom. Panic attacks can be triggered by specific situations or can occur unexpectedly, leading to a fear of having another attack.

3. **Social Anxiety Disorder (SAD)**: SAD, also known as social phobia, involves an intense fear of being embarrassed, judged, or humiliated in social situations. People with SAD may avoid social interactions or endure them with extreme distress. Physical symptoms can include blushing, sweating, trembling, rapid heartbeat, and nausea. Common triggers for SAD can

include public speaking, meeting new people, or being the center of attention.

4. **Specific Phobias:** This refers to an intense and irrational fear of a particular object, situation, or activity. Common phobias include fear of heights, spiders, flying, or enclosed spaces. When exposed to the phobic stimulus, individuals may experience immediate anxiety or panic attacks. Avoidance of the feared object or situation is a typical response. Triggers for specific phobias are unique to each individual's specific fear.

These are just brief explanations of the types of anxiety disorders mentioned. Each person's experience with anxiety disorders can vary, and a proper diagnosis and treatment plan should be discussed with a healthcare professional.

Cognitive distortions play a significant role in anxiety disorders. CBT addresses these. These are distorted thought patterns that contribute to negative emotions and anxious feelings. Examples of cognitive distortions include catastrophizing, overgeneralizing, and black-and-white thinking. By identifying and challenging these distortions, you can gain a clearer perspective and reduce anxiety.

Three Effective CBT Methods to Control Anxiety

Cognitive Behavioral Therapy (CBT) has proven to be effective in managing various mental health conditions, including anxiety. Here, we will explore three specific CBT methods that can help individuals gain control over their anxiety levels. These methods include cognitive restructuring, exposure therapy, and relaxation techniques, each offering different strategies to challenge anxious thoughts, face fears, and promote relaxation.

1. Cognitive Restructuring for Anxiety

To effectively address anxiety in Cognitive Behavioral Therapy (CBT), it's crucial to identify and challenge the anxious thoughts that contribute to excessive fear and worry.

One important step in identifying anxious thoughts is recognizing cognitive distortions. These are patterns of thinking that can lead to inaccurate perceptions of reality and exacerbate anxiety. They often involve making inaccurate assumptions or jumping to negative conclusions without concrete evidence.

Recognizing these cognitive distortions is the first step in challenging and replacing them with more rational thoughts. By questioning the accuracy of your negative thoughts and looking for evidence to support or refute them, you can reduce anxiety and develop a more balanced and realistic outlook.

Remember, it takes practice and patience to overcome these patterns of thinking, but with time, you can cultivate a more positive and rational mindset.

Step 1: Understand Cognitive Distortions
- Familiarize yourself with common cognitive distortions, which are irrational or inaccurate ways of thinking that

contribute to anxiety. Examples include all-or-nothing thinking, overgeneralization, and catastrophizing.
- Educate yourself on the different types of cognitive distortions and how they may manifest in your thoughts.

Step 2: Identify Anxious Thoughts
- Pay attention to your thoughts and notice when you feel anxious.
- Start keeping a thought record or journal to document your anxious thoughts. Write down the situations that trigger anxiety and the thoughts that accompany them.

Step 3: Recognize Cognitive Distortions
- Review your thought record and look for patterns or themes in your anxious thoughts.
- Identify any cognitive distortions present in your thinking. For each anxious thought, ask yourself if any cognitive distortions might be influencing that thought.

Step 4: Challenge Cognitive Distortions
- Once you have identified a cognitive distortion, challenge it by questioning its validity. Ask yourself if there is evidence to support or contradict the distorted thought.
- Consider alternative explanations or perspectives that are more realistic and balanced.
- Look for evidence that contradicts the distorted thought and write it down.

Step 5: Cognitive Restructuring
- Replace the distorted thought with a more rational and balanced one. This process is called cognitive restructuring.
- Write down the new thought that challenges the distortion and offers a more realistic perspective.
- Repeat this new thought to yourself whenever the distorted thought resurfaces.

Step 6: Practice Self-Compassion
- Recognize that challenging anxious thoughts and cognitive distortions take time and practice.
- Be patient with yourself and show self-compassion throughout this process.
- Celebrate your progress and acknowledge the effort you are putting into managing your anxiety.

Step 7: Seek Professional Help if Needed
- If your anxiety persists or becomes overwhelming, consider seeking help from a mental health professional.
- They can provide additional support, guidance, and techniques specific to your needs.

Remember, challenging anxious thoughts and cognitive distortions is an ongoing process. With practice, you can develop healthier thinking patterns and better manage your anxiety.

2. Relaxation and Stress Management Techniques

To manage your anxiety and continue on your journey toward emotional freedom and inner peace, it's essential to incorporate relaxation and stress management techniques into your daily routine. These techniques can help you reduce stress, calm your mind, and promote a sense of well-being.

There are various methods you can try, such as deep breathing, progressive muscle relaxation, guided imagery, mindfulness meditation, and stress reduction exercises.

> ### Deep Breathing
>
> **Deep breathing** is a simple yet powerful technique that can be done anywhere, anytime. Deep breathing exercises are an effective technique for managing anxiety and promoting relaxation.
>
> 1. **Find a quiet and comfortable space:** Choose a peaceful environment where you can relax without distractions. Sit in a chair or on the floor, ensuring your back is straight but not tense.
>
> 2. **Relax your body:** Close your eyes and take a moment to release any tension in your body. Start by loosening your jaw, relaxing your shoulders, and allowing your muscles to unwind.

3. **Take a deep breath in:** Inhale slowly through your nose, counting to four in your mind. Focus on filling your lungs completely with air, expanding your diaphragm as you breathe in.

4. **Hold your breath:** Once you've taken a deep breath, hold it gently for a count of four. This pause allows you to fully absorb the oxygen and engage in a mindful moment.

5. **Exhale slowly:** Begin exhaling slowly through your mouth, counting to four. As you release the air, imagine letting go of any tension or anxious thoughts. Aim to make your exhale longer than your inhale, as this activates the relaxation response.

6. **Repeat the cycle:** Inhale again, following the same count of four. Continue the cycle of inhaling, holding, and exhaling for a few minutes or until you start feeling more relaxed and centered.

Tips for Enhancing Effectiveness:

1. **Practice regularly:** Consistency is key when it comes to deep breathing exercises. Set aside a few minutes each day to practice, and gradually increase the duration as you become more comfortable.

2. **Focus on your breath:** Direct your attention solely on your breath during the exercise. If your mind wanders, gently bring your focus back to your breathing without judgment.

3. **Engage your diaphragm:** Deep breathing involves the use of your diaphragm, so make sure you're breathing deeply into your belly rather than shallowly into your chest. Place your hand on your abdomen to feel it rise and fall with each breath.

4. **Combine with visualization or affirmations:** While practicing deep breathing, you can enhance its effectiveness by visualizing a peaceful scene or repeating calming affirmations in your mind. This can further promote relaxation and reduce anxiety.

5. **Practice mindfulness**: Deep breathing exercises can be a form of mindfulness. As you breathe, try to fully experience the present moment, observing your thoughts and sensations without judgment.

Progressive Muscle Relaxation

Progressive muscle relaxation involves tensing and then releasing different muscle groups in your body.

1. Find a quiet and comfortable place to sit or lie down. Close your eyes and take a few deep breaths to relax your mind and body.

2. Start with your toes. Tense the muscles in your toes by curling them downwards. Hold this tension for 5 to 10 seconds, then release and let the tension flow out. Focus on the feeling of relaxation in your toes.

3. Move up to your feet. Flex your feet by pointing your toes towards your head. Hold this tension for 5 to 10 seconds, then release and feel the relaxation spreading through your feet.

4. Tense your calf muscles. Pull your toes towards your body, tensing your calf muscles. Hold for 5 to 10 seconds, then release and notice the sensation of relaxation in your calves.

5. Tense your thigh muscles. Tighten your thigh muscles by pushing your knees together. Hold for 5 to 10 seconds, then release and feel the tension melting away.

6. Move up to your abdomen. Take a deep breath in and tighten your stomach muscles. Hold for 5 to 10 seconds, then exhale and let go of the tension, feeling the relaxation in your abdomen.

7. Tense your chest muscles. Take another deep breath in and hold it. Tighten your chest muscles as you hold your breath for 5 to 10 seconds. Exhale slowly, releasing the tension and allowing your chest to relax.

8. Move to your shoulders. Shrug your shoulders up towards your ears, creating tension in your shoulder muscles. Hold for 5 to 10 seconds, then release and let your shoulders drop, feeling the relaxation spreading across your upper body.

9. Tense your arms. Make fists with your hands and flex your biceps, creating tension in your arms. Hold for 5 to 10 seconds, then release and let your arms go limp, noticing the sensation of relaxation in your arms.

10. Move to your neck. Gently tilt your head back and feel the stretch in your neck muscles. Hold for 5 to 10 seconds, then release and let your head return to its natural position, feeling the tension release from your neck.

11. Finally, focus on your face. Scrunch up your face tightly, wrinkling your forehead, and squeezing your eyes shut. Hold for 5 to 10 seconds, then release and let your face relax completely.

Tips to make this exercise more effective:

1. **Practice deep breathing:** Take slow, deep breaths throughout the exercise to enhance relaxation and oxygenate your body.

2. **Visualize tension leaving your body:** As you release each muscle group, imagine the tension flowing out of your body and being replaced with a sense of calm and relaxation.

3. **Use calming imagery:** Visualize yourself in a peaceful and serene environment, such as a beach or a forest, to enhance relaxation and distract your mind from anxious thoughts.

4. **Practice regularly:** Aim to do this exercise for at least 10-15 minutes each day or whenever you feel anxious. Consistency

will help you develop a deeper sense of relaxation and make it easier to release tension in your body.

5. **Combine with other relaxation techniques:** Progressive muscle relaxation can be even more effective when combined with other relaxation techniques, such as guided imagery, meditation, or listening to calming music.

6. **Seek professional guidance:** If you have severe anxiety or if this exercise doesn't provide sufficient relief, consider seeking guidance from a mental health professional who can provide additional support and techniques tailored to your specific needs.

Guided Imagery

Guided imagery involves using your imagination to create a peaceful and calming mental image.

1. Find a quiet and comfortable space where you can relax without any distractions. Sit or lie down in a comfortable position.

2. Close your eyes and take a few deep breaths to relax your body and mind. Inhale deeply through your nose, hold for a few seconds, and exhale slowly through your mouth. Repeat this a few times until you feel calm and centered.

3. Begin to visualize your serene place. It could be a beach, a forest, a meadow, or any location that brings you a sense of peace and tranquility. Imagine the details of this place, including the colors, shapes, and textures.

4. Engage your senses by focusing on the sounds in your serene place. Imagine the sound of the waves crashing on the shore, the rustling of leaves in the forest, or the chirping of birds. Try to make these sounds as vivid and realistic as possible.

5. Now, shift your focus to the scents of your serene place. Imagine the smell of the salty ocean breeze, the earthy aroma of the forest, or the sweet fragrance of flowers. Take a moment to inhale deeply and experience these scents in your imagination.

6. Explore the sensations in your serene place. Feel the warmth of the sun on your skin, the coolness of the shade under a tree, or the softness of the sand beneath your feet. Imagine these sensations and allow yourself to fully experience them in your mind.

7. As you continue to immerse yourself in this imagery, let go of any stress, worries, or negative thoughts. Imagine them being washed away by the waves or dissolving into the air. Focus on the serenity of your surroundings and allow yourself to feel a sense of calm and relaxation.

Tips for Making this Exercise More Effective:

1. Practice deep breathing throughout the exercise to enhance relaxation.

2. Use visualization techniques to make the imagery more vivid. Imagine vibrant colors, clear sounds, and realistic sensations.

3. Engage all your senses to fully immerse yourself in the experience. Visualize, hear, smell, and feel your serene place as vividly as possible.

4. If your mind starts to wander or negative thoughts arise, gently bring your focus back to the imagery. Don't judge yourself for any distractions. Simply refocus on your serene place.

5. Practice this exercise regularly, even when you're not feeling anxious, to strengthen your ability to relax and find inner peace.

Remember, guided imagery is a personal experience, so feel free to modify this exercise to suit your preferences and needs.

Mindfulness Meditation

Mindfulness meditation is about being fully present in the moment, without judgment.

Find a quiet space, sit comfortably, and focus your attention on your breath. Notice the sensations of each inhale and exhale, and whenever your mind wanders, gently bring it back to your breath. This practice can help you cultivate a sense of calm and centeredness.

Mindfulness Exercise for Anxiety: Focusing on Breath

1. Find a Quiet Space: Choose a calm and quiet environment where you can sit comfortably without distractions. This could be a quiet room, a peaceful outdoor spot, or any place where you feel at ease.

2. Sit Comfortably: Find a comfortable position, either sitting on a chair with your feet flat on the ground or sitting cross-legged on a cushion. Keep your back straight but relaxed, allowing for a natural flow of breath.

3. Settle In: Take a moment to settle into your body and surroundings. Close your eyes or keep them softly focused on a point in front of you. Begin to bring your attention to the present moment.

4. Focus on Your Breath: Shift your attention to your breath without trying to change it in any way. Notice the sensation of the breath as it enters and leaves your body. Pay attention to how it feels in your nose, throat, chest, or abdomen.

5. Be Curious: Observe the breath with curiosity, as if you are discovering it for the first time. Notice the rhythm, depth, and quality of each inhalation and exhalation. Be fully present with each breath.

6. Acknowledge Thoughts and Let Them Go: As thoughts arise (and they will), gently acknowledge them without judgment or engagement. Let them pass by like clouds in the sky, allowing your attention to return to your breath.

7. Cultivate Non-Judgmental Awareness: If you notice any judgments or evaluations about your practice or thoughts, simply acknowledge them and gently let them go. Remind yourself that this exercise is about observing and accepting your experience as it is.

8. Practice Patience: Be patient and compassionate with yourself. Your mind may wander frequently, especially in the beginning. Whenever you notice your mind has wandered, gently guide your attention back to the breath.

Tips for Making this Exercise More Effective:

1. **Consistency:** Set aside a regular time each day to practice this exercise. Consistency will help you establish a habit and deepen your mindfulness practice.

2. **Start with Short Sessions:** Begin with shorter sessions, such as 5 to 10 minutes, and gradually increase the duration as you feel more comfortable and grounded in the practice.

3. **Use Guided Meditations:** If you find it challenging to stay focused, consider using guided meditation apps or recordings. These can provide helpful instructions and support during your practice.

4. **Expand Beyond Formal Practice:** Bring mindfulness into your everyday life by incorporating short moments of focusing on your breath throughout the day. Take a few mindful breaths during transitions or when you feel overwhelmed.

Be patient, kind, and gentle with yourself as you cultivate a sense of calm and centeredness through this mindfulness exercise.

Incorporating these relaxation and stress management techniques into your daily routine can make a significant difference in your overall well-being. Take time for yourself each day, even if it's just for a few minutes, to practice these techniques. As you become more familiar with them, you'll find that you're better able to manage stress, reduce anxiety, and experience greater emotional freedom and inner peace.

3. Exposure Therapy and Desensitization Techniques

To overcome anxiety and address the anxious thoughts identified in the previous subtopic, you can utilize exposure therapy and desensitization techniques.

These methods are effective in helping you gradually confront and overcome your fears, enabling you to live a happier, healthier life.

Exposure therapy involves facing your fears in a controlled and systematic way. By gradually exposing yourself to the situations or objects that trigger your anxiety, you can gradually build up your tolerance and reduce your fear response. This process is known as systematic desensitization.

In recent years, virtual reality therapy has emerged as a powerful tool in exposure therapy. This technology allows you to experience realistic simulations of your fears in a safe and controlled environment. By immersing yourself in these virtual scenarios, you can practice facing your fears and develop coping strategies without the risk associated with real-life exposure. Virtual reality therapy can be particularly beneficial for individuals with specific phobias or PTSD.

Exposure therapy is a proven method for reducing anxiety by gradually exposing oneself to feared situations or stimuli. However, it is essential to approach exposure therapy with caution and follow certain guidelines to ensure safety and effectiveness. This step-by-step guide will assist you in practicing exposure therapy and desensitization for anxiety in a safe and manageable manner.

Start small. Begin with situations or stimuli that evoke mild anxiety. It is crucial to start with manageable challenges and gradually progress to more anxiety-provoking scenarios. Exposure therapy may not be suitable for everyone, and it is important to consult with a qualified mental health professional before starting. They can provide personalized guidance and support throughout the process.

Step 1: Identify the Fear or Trigger

Identify the specific fear or trigger you want to address. It could be a situation, object, or activity that causes anxiety.

Step 2: Create a Hierarchy
Create a hierarchy of anxiety-inducing situations or stimuli related to your fear. Arrange them in order from least to most anxiety-provoking. This will help you plan your exposure practices gradually.

Step 3: Relaxation Techniques
Before starting exposure, learn and practice relaxation techniques such as deep breathing, progressive muscle relaxation, or mindfulness. These techniques will help you manage anxiety during exposure exercises.

Step 4: Exposure Practice
a. Start with the least anxiety-provoking situation or stimulus from your hierarchy.
b. Visualize the situation or view pictures/videos of the stimulus if applicable.
c. Gradually expose yourself to the situation or stimulus in real life, if possible. Start with short durations and gradually increase the exposure time.
d. As you engage with the fear-inducing situation or stimulus, practice your relaxation techniques to manage anxiety.
e. Repeat the exposure exercise until your anxiety decreases significantly (around 50 to 70% reduction) before moving to the next step in the hierarchy.

Step 5: Generalization
Once you can successfully manage anxiety in one situation or with one stimulus, repeat the exposure exercise with similar

but slightly different situations or stimuli. This will help generalize your anxiety management skills.

Step 6: Maintain Regular Exposure Practices
Continuously challenge yourself by revisiting previously encountered anxiety-provoking situations or stimuli. Regular exposure practice helps maintain progress and prevent regression.

Tips for Effective and Safe Practice:

1. **Patience is key.** Remember that progress may take time. Be patient and celebrate even small achievements.

2. **Stay within your comfort zone.** Pushing yourself too hard can lead to overwhelming anxiety. Gradually increase exposure difficulty only when you feel ready.

3. **Practice self-compassion.** Be kind to yourself throughout the process. Acknowledge your efforts and reward yourself for taking steps towards managing anxiety.

4. **Seek support.** Engage with a mental health professional or consider joining a support group to share experiences, gain insights, and receive guidance during your exposure therapy journey.

> **Warning!**
>
> 1. If at any point during exposure exercises, you experience severe distress, panic attacks, or significant impairment in functioning, discontinue the exercise and seek professional help.
>
> 2. Exposure therapy may not be suitable for individuals with certain mental health conditions or trauma-related issues. Consult with a mental health professional to determine the appropriateness of exposure therapy for your specific situation.
>
> 3. Ensure your safety during exposure practice. Avoid engaging in exposure exercises that may put you at risk of harm or injury.

Exposure therapy and desensitization can be effective tools for managing anxiety. By following this step-by-step guide and adhering to the necessary precautions, you can gradually overcome anxiety-inducing situations or stimuli and improve your overall well-being.

Developing Effective Coping Mechanisms for Anxiety

Even while anxiety can be crippling, you can learn to deal with it and come out on the other side stronger and more resilient with the right tools and approaches. Use the strategies listed above as a coping mechanism to deal with anxiety when it strikes or to stop it from creating havoc in your life.

Developing effective coping mechanisms for anxiety involves a combination of self-awareness, experimentation, and consistency. Remember, developing coping mechanisms takes time and practice. Be patient with yourself as you explore different techniques and find what works best for you. With effective coping mechanisms in your arsenal, you can conquer anxiety and discover inner peace.

In the garden of life, anxiety can be seen as a wild weed that has the potential to suffocate the beautiful flowers of joy. However, it's important to remember that even the most fragile petals are capable of enduring the harshest storms. Embrace the uncertainties that come your way, as they provide the nourishment needed for the resilient roots that reside deep within your soul.

Allow your spirit to soar above the dark clouds of worry. While anxiety may accompany you on your journey, it will never determine your destination.

Chapter 4
Curing OCD with CBT

Are you struggling with OCD and intrusive thoughts? You're not alone. The constant bombardment of unwanted thoughts can feel overwhelming and exhausting. But there's hope. With the help of Cognitive Behavioral Therapy (CBT) techniques, you can conquer OCD and regain control over your thoughts and your life.

In the case of OCD and intrusive thoughts, CBT can be highly effective because it addresses the underlying cognitive distortions and maladaptive behaviors that maintain the disorder.

CBT for OCD typically involves two main components: cognitive restructuring and exposure and response prevention (ERP)

CBT for OCD is considered the gold standard treatment and has been extensively researched and proven effective. It empowers individuals to develop skills to manage their thoughts and urges, allowing them to regain control over their lives and reduce the impact of OCD on their daily functioning.

It is important to note that seeking professional help from a trained therapist is highly recommended when dealing with OCD and intrusive thoughts. They can provide guidance and support throughout the CBT process, tailoring the treatment to individual needs and ensuring the best possible outcome.

Understanding Obsessive-Compulsive Disorder (OCD)

OCD is a mental health condition characterized by persistent and unwanted thoughts (obsessions) and the urge to perform repetitive behaviors (compulsions) in an attempt to alleviate anxiety or prevent a feared outcome.

Obsessions are intrusive and persistent thoughts, urges, or images that cause distress. These thoughts are often irrational and go against a person's values or beliefs. Common obsessions include fears of contamination, the need for symmetry or order, taboo or aggressive thoughts, and a constant need for reassurance.

Compulsions are repetitive behaviors or mental acts that individuals with OCD feel compelled to perform in response to their obsessions. These compulsions are aimed at reducing anxiety or preventing a feared event from occurring. Examples of compulsions may include excessive handwashing, checking locks repeatedly, counting or repeating specific words, or arranging objects in a particular way.

People with OCD often experience a cycle of obsessions and compulsions. The obsessions create intense anxiety and discomfort, leading to the performance of compulsions as a means of temporary relief. However, this relief is short-lived, and the cycle repeats, causing significant distress and interference with daily functioning.

The exact cause of OCD is not fully understood. It is believed to be a combination of genetic, neurological, and environmental factors. Research suggests that imbalances in certain brain chemicals, such as serotonin, may play a role. Traumatic life events, such as abuse or loss, may also contribute to the development of OCD in some individuals.

Living with OCD can be challenging and exhausting. Individuals with OCD often describe feeling trapped in their own minds and unable to control their thoughts and behaviors. They may experience intense anxiety, guilt, and shame due to the irrational nature of their obsessions. The constant need to engage in compulsions can be time-consuming and interfere with work, relationships, and daily activities. Additionally, the stigma surrounding mental health can add to the burden and make seeking help difficult.

It is important to note that OCD is a treatable condition. Cognitive-behavioral therapy (CBT), particularly exposure and response prevention (ERP), is considered the gold-standard treatment for OCD. Medications, such as selective serotonin reuptake inhibitors (SSRIs), may also be prescribed to help manage symptoms. Seeking professional help from a mental health provider is crucial for individuals struggling with OCD to receive an accurate diagnosis and appropriate treatment.

Three Major Approaches for Treating OCD

There are many different ways to manage OCD, and cognitive behavioral therapy (CBT) is one of the most successful strategies that can be used in conjunction with others. These are some of the most effective CBT strategies that deliver significant changes in manageable steps that you may practice to become a regular part of your life and conduct on your own to prevent OCD symptoms from taking over your life.

1. Practicing Cognitive Flexibility

To effectively manage OCD symptoms and promote lasting change, you can employ these specific cognitive restructuring techniques as part of your Cognitive Behavioral Therapy (CBT) journey.

One of the key OCD management techniques in cognitive restructuring is practicing cognitive flexibility. This involves learning to view your thoughts and fears from different perspectives. Instead of getting stuck in rigid thinking patterns, you can learn to challenge the validity of your obsessive thoughts and question the need for your compulsive behaviors. By practicing cognitive flexibility, you can develop a more balanced and realistic view of your fears, reducing anxiety and allowing for more adaptive responses.

Step 1: Identify the Obsessive Thought
The first step in practicing cognitive flexibility is to identify the specific obsessive thought that you want to challenge. This

could be a recurring fear, doubt, or worry that is causing distress and leading to compulsive behaviors.

> **Example:** Let's say the obsessive thought is a fear of contamination, causing excessive hand washing.

Step 2: Question the Evidence

Once you have identified the obsessive thought, start questioning the evidence that supports it. Ask yourself if there is any real evidence to support the validity of this thought. Is it based on facts, or is it just a perception or assumption?

> **Example:** Ask yourself, *"Is there any tangible evidence that my hands are actually contaminated? Am I assuming they are dirty without any real proof?"*

Step 3: Consider Alternative Explanations

Next, consider alternative explanations for the obsessive thought. Are there other possible interpretations or reasons for the thought? This step involves actively seeking different perspectives and possibilities.

> **Example:** Consider the possibility that your hands may not be contaminated at all. Could it be that your fear is a result of anxiety rather than actual contamination?

Step 4: Evaluate the Consequences

Evaluate the consequences of continuing to believe in the obsessive thought. Consider how it impacts your daily life, relationships, and overall well-being. Reflect on whether holding onto this thought is helpful or harmful.

> **Example:** Reflect on how excessive hand washing is affecting your skin, relationships, and time management. Is the compulsive behavior bringing you relief or causing more distress?

Step 5: Challenge the Thought

Once you have questioned the evidence, considered alternative explanations, and evaluated the consequences, it's time to challenge the validity of the obsessive thought. Look for evidence that contradicts or undermines the thought. Seek out logical and rational reasons to counteract the obsessive belief.

> **Example:** Challenge the thought of contamination by reminding yourself of instances where you didn't get sick despite not washing your hands excessively. Reflect on how many times you have touched things without negative consequences.

Step 6: Reframe the Thought

Reframe the obsessive thought to create a more balanced and realistic perspective. Replace the irrational belief with a more rational and evidence-based thought. This step involves finding a middle ground between the extreme thoughts and finding a more reasonable standpoint.

> **Example:** Reframe the thought by telling yourself, *"While it's important to maintain good hygiene, excessive hand washing is unnecessary. I can practice reasonable hygiene without letting fear control my actions."*

Step 7: Practice Mindfulness and Acceptance

Finally, practice mindfulness and acceptance of obsessive thoughts without engaging in compulsive behaviors. Acknowledge the thought without judgment, allowing it to come and go without acting on it.

> **Example:** Instead of immediately washing your hands, take a moment to observe the thought, acknowledge it as just a thought, and let it pass without giving in to the compulsion.

This process helps reduce anxiety and allows for more adaptive responses to the thoughts and fears associated with OCD. It may take time and effort to fully incorporate cognitive flexibility into your OCD management routine, so be patient and persistent.

2. Using Anxiety Reduction Methods

Another important aspect of cognitive restructuring is using anxiety reduction methods. These techniques help you reduce the intensity of your anxiety, making it easier to challenge your OCD thoughts and behaviors.

Deep breathing exercises, progressive muscle relaxation, and mindfulness meditation are just a few examples of anxiety reduction methods that can be incorporated into your daily routine to promote relaxation and emotional well-being.

1. **Deep Breathing:** Find a quiet and comfortable place to sit or lie down. Close your eyes and take a slow, deep breath in through your nose, filling your lungs completely. Hold your breath for a few seconds, then slowly exhale through your mouth. Repeat this deep breathing exercise for several minutes, focusing on the sensation of your breath entering and leaving your body. Deep breathing helps activate the body's relaxation response, reducing anxiety.

2. **Progressive Muscle Relaxation:** Start by tensing and then relaxing each muscle group in your body, one at a time. Begin with your toes, then move up to your feet, calves, thighs, abdomen, chest, arms, hands, neck, and finally your face and scalp. As you tense each muscle group, hold the tension for a few seconds, then release and let the muscles relax completely. This technique helps to release tension and promote a sense of calm.

3. **Guided Imagery:** Find a quiet space where you won't be disturbed. Close your eyes and imagine yourself in a peaceful and calming environment, such as a beach or a forest. Engage all your senses by imagining the sights, sounds, smells, and textures of this place. Spend a few minutes fully immersing yourself in this mental image, allowing it to replace anxious thoughts and create a sense of relaxation.

4. **Mindfulness Meditation:** Sit comfortably and focus your attention on your breath. Be fully present in the moment, observing your thoughts and sensations without judgment. If your mind wanders, gently bring your attention back to your breath. Practice mindfulness meditation for a few minutes each day, gradually increasing the duration over time. This technique helps reduce anxiety by promoting a non-reactive and accepting mindset.

5. **Physical Exercise:** Regular physical activity, such as walking, jogging, or dancing, can help reduce anxiety. Exercise releases endorphins, which are natural mood-boosting chemicals in the brain. To experience the benefits, aim for at least 30 minutes of moderate-intensity exercise most days of the week.

6. **Challenge Negative Thoughts:** Identify and challenge any negative or irrational thoughts that contribute to your anxiety. Write them down and evaluate the evidence for and against these thoughts. Replace them with more realistic and positive thoughts.

7. **Social Support:** Reach out to trusted friends, family members, or support groups who can provide understanding and encouragement. Sharing your thoughts and feelings with others who can relate can help alleviate anxiety.

8. **Limit Stressors:** Take steps to reduce stress in your life. Identify any sources of stress and develop strategies to minimize or manage them. This may involve setting boundaries, prioritizing self-care, and practicing relaxation techniques regularly.

9. **Healthy Lifestyle:** Maintain a balanced diet, get adequate sleep, and limit caffeine and alcohol intake. A healthy lifestyle can have a positive impact on anxiety levels.

10. **Seek Professional Help:** If anxiety persists or becomes overwhelming, consider seeking professional help. A mental health professional, such as a therapist or psychiatrist, can provide guidance, support, and additional tools for managing anxiety and challenging OCD thoughts and behaviors.

Anxiety reduction techniques can be helpful in making it easier to challenge OCD thoughts by helping individuals manage and lower their overall anxiety levels. When anxiety is high, it can be difficult to engage in rational thinking and challenge the irrational thoughts associated with OCD.

3. Exposure and Response Prevention (ERP) Techniques for OCD

Exposure and response prevention, also known as ERP, is a powerful tool for reducing anxiety and breaking free from the cycle of obsessions and compulsions.

Exposure therapy is a key component of ERP. It involves gradually exposing yourself to situations or thoughts that trigger your OCD. By confronting these triggers in a safe and controlled way, you can learn to tolerate the anxiety they produce without resorting to compulsive behaviors. This process allows your brain to rewire itself and create new, healthier connections.

An important aspect of exposure therapy is **anxiety management**. As you face your fears, it's normal to experience heightened anxiety. Learning effective strategies to manage and reduce anxiety can make the process more manageable. Techniques such as deep breathing, progressive muscle relaxation, and mindfulness can help you stay grounded and focused during exposure exercises.

Thought-stopping is another ERP technique. It involves consciously interrupting obsessive thoughts and redirecting attention to a more positive or neutral focus. This technique helps break the cycle of rumination and reduces the power of obsessions over the mind.

Whenever you notice an obsessive thought or urge, you can use a simple phrase like *'Stop!'* or *'No!'* to interrupt the thought pattern. This technique helps you regain control over your thinking and prevents the obsession from escalating into a full-blown compulsion.

Habit reversal is a crucial aspect of response prevention in ERP. It involves identifying and replacing compulsive behaviors with healthier alternatives. By becoming aware of your compulsions and actively choosing not to engage in them, you can weaken their grip on your life.

Desensitization techniques are also employed in ERP. These involve gradually increasing the intensity of exposure to triggers over time. By repeatedly exposing yourself to situations that provoke anxiety, you can desensitize your brain and reduce the fear response associated with those triggers.

Here is a sample OCD Management Program is designed to provide a structured and easy-to-follow approach to managing Obsessive-Compulsive Disorder (OCD) symptoms through Cognitive-Behavioral Therapy (CBT) techniques. The program emphasizes exposure therapy, anxiety management, thought-stopping, habit reversal, and desensitization to effectively target OCD symptoms. The primary goal is to reduce the impact of OCD on daily functioning and improve overall quality of life.

Program Structure:
The program is divided into three phases, each building upon the previous one to gradually increase exposure to anxiety-provoking situations and promote habit reversal. It is recommended to spend approximately 2 to 3 weeks on each phase, but the duration may vary based on individual progress.

Phase 1: Psychoeducation and Anxiety Management
- Education about OCD and the CBT model
- Identifying and tracking OCD symptoms and triggers
- Learning relaxation techniques (e.g., deep breathing, progressive muscle relaxation)
- Developing an anxiety hierarchy, ranking anxiety-inducing situations from least to most distressing

Phase 2: Exposure Therapy and Response Prevention
- Gradual exposure to anxiety-provoking situations from the hierarchy
- Encouraging the individual to confront obsessions and resist engaging in compulsions

- Implementing response prevention techniques (e.g., delaying, distraction, thought stopping)
- Guided imagery and visualization exercises to enhance exposure

Phase 3: Habit Reversal and Maintenance
- Identifying and challenging OCD-related thoughts and beliefs
- Implementing habit reversal techniques to replace compulsions with healthier behaviors
- Developing coping strategies to manage setbacks and relapse prevention
- Promoting self-monitoring of symptoms and progress

Note: Personalize this program based on individual needs and consult a qualified mental health professional for guidance and support. This program serves as a general guideline and should be adapted as necessary.

Remember, consistency, patience, and perseverance are key to achieving long-term success in managing OCD symptoms.

Create a Structured Plan for Overcoming OCD

Overcoming Obsessive-Compulsive Disorder (OCD) requires a structured plan that combines cognitive restructuring techniques and Exposure and Response Prevention (ERP). It is important to keep in mind a few considerations.

Firstly, familiarize yourself with the symptoms and nature of OCD to gain a better understanding of the disorder. This knowledge will help you approach your treatment with a clearer perspective. Secondly, seeking guidance from a qualified mental health professional who specializes in OCD treatment is highly recommended. They can tailor the plan to your specific needs and provide you with the necessary support throughout the process. Lastly, remember that overcoming OCD takes time and effort. Be patient with yourself and remain persistent in practicing the techniques above.

To all those who suffer in the relentless grip of OCD, I want you to know that you are not alone in this battle. The challenges you face may seem overwhelming, but within you lies a strength that is unyielding. Remember that you are so much more than your intrusive thoughts and compulsions.

Your resilience is inspiring, and your courage in facing each day with unwavering determination is commendable. As you embark on your journey of managing OCD through CBT, know that it won't be easy, but with every step forward, you are reclaiming control over your life.

Embrace the therapeutic tools and strategies that CBT offers, for they hold the promise of liberation from the chains that bind you. Be patient with yourself, for healing takes time, and remember to celebrate even the smallest victories along the way. Reach out for support when needed, for there are those who understand and empathize with your struggles.

Trust in the process, believe in your ability to overcome and know that a brighter future awaits you. You are strong, you are resilient, and you are deserving of a life filled with peace, joy, and freedom.

Chapter 5
Treating Addiction with CBT

If you're struggling with addiction, CBT can be a highly effective approach to help you regain control of your life and overcome destructive behaviors. Treating substance abuse with cognitive behavioral therapy (CBT) involves using specific techniques to address the underlying thoughts, beliefs, and behaviors that contribute to addiction. By targeting these cognitive factors, CBT aims to help you break free from the cycle of dependency and achieve lasting recovery.

For example, let's consider a hypothetical case of someone struggling with alcohol addiction. Through CBT, the individual would work with a therapist to identify the thoughts and situations that lead to their alcohol use. They may discover that they often have the belief that they "need" alcohol to relax or have fun. The therapist would help the individual challenge this belief by exploring alternative ways to relax or have fun without relying on alcohol. They may also work on developing healthier coping strategies, such as engaging in hobbies or seeking support from friends and family.

CBT for addiction typically involves several key components:

CBT for Addiction Key Components

1. Psychoeducation Educate the individual about addiction, its underlying causes, and the role of thoughts and beliefs in maintaining addictive behaviors.
2. Functional Analysis You can work together with a therapist to identify the triggers, thoughts, and emotions that contribute to substance abuse. This helps the individual gain insight into the patterns of their addiction.
3. Cognitive Restructuring Identify and challenge their negative thoughts and beliefs related to substance abuse. Develop more positive and realistic ways of thinking.
4. Skills Training The individual learns practical skills and strategies to cope with cravings, manage stress, and resist the temptation to use substances. These skills are reinforced through practice and homework assignments during therapy.
5. Relapse Prevention Develop a relapse prevention plan, which includes identifying high-risk situations, developing coping strategies, and creating a support network.

Note: CBT for addiction may not work for everyone, and individual outcomes vary. Factors such as the severity of addiction, co-occurring mental health conditions, and an individual's motivation and commitment to change can influence the effectiveness of CBT. Additionally, CBT may be more effective when combined with other treatment approaches, such as medication-assisted therapy or support groups.

Disclaimers:

- **Not a Cure:** CBT for addiction is not a one-size-fits-all solution or a cure for addiction. It is a therapeutic approach that can assist individuals in changing their thoughts and behaviors related to substance abuse, but it requires ongoing effort and commitment.
- **Individual Variations:** Results may vary depending on the individual and their unique circumstances. Some individuals may experience significant improvements, while others may require additional or alternative treatment approaches.
- **Co-occurring Disorders:** CBT may be less effective for individuals with severe mental health conditions, such as schizophrenia or bipolar disorder, as these conditions may require specialized treatment approaches. In such cases, a comprehensive treatment plan that addresses both addiction and mental health is recommended.

CBT is a valuable treatment approach for addiction that focuses on changing negative thought patterns and behaviors associated with substance abuse. While it may not work for everyone, it has shown promising results for many individuals seeking recovery. However, it is important to consult with a professional to assess the suitability of CBT for each individual case and to consider other treatment options if needed.

Cognitive Interventions for Addiction

Cognitive behavioral therapy (CBT) is a widely used therapeutic approach for various mental health conditions, including addiction, depression, anxiety, and OCD. While the basic principles of CBT remain the same across these different issues, there are some specific cognitive interventions that differentiate CBT for addiction from CBT for other conditions.

1. Cognitive Restructuring

CBT for addiction:
Cognitive restructuring focuses on challenging and changing distorted beliefs and cognitions related to substance use. This involves identifying and modifying thoughts that support addictive behaviors, such as rationalizations or beliefs about the benefits of substance use.

CBT for depression, anxiety, and OCD:
It may involve restructuring negative or irrational thoughts related to self-worth, danger, or obsessions.

2. Craving Management

CBT for addiction:
Often includes specific techniques to manage cravings, which are intense urges to use substances. These techniques involve identifying triggers, developing coping strategies, and learning to tolerate and manage cravings effectively.

3. Relapse Prevention

CBT for addiction:
Given the chronic nature of addiction, CBT for addiction places significant emphasis on relapse prevention. Specific interventions focus on identifying high-risk situations, developing coping skills, and creating a relapse prevention plan.

CBT for depression, anxiety, or OCD:
This aspect is not as prominent in CBT for depression, anxiety, or OCD, where relapse is not typically a central concern.

4. Motivational Enhancement

CBT for addiction:
Often incorporates motivational enhancement techniques to increase motivation for change. This involves exploring and resolving ambivalence towards substance use and building intrinsic motivation to quit or reduce substance abuse.

CBT for depression, anxiety, or OCD:
Motivational enhancement is less commonly utilized in CBT for depression, anxiety, or OCD, where motivation is usually assumed to be present.

5. Addressing Lifestyle Factors

CBT for addiction:
Recognizes that addiction is influenced by various lifestyle factors, such as social environment, relationships, and daily routines. Interventions may involve identifying and modifying these factors to support recovery.

CBT for other conditions:
While lifestyle factors may also be addressed in CBT for other conditions, the focus is more specific to addiction treatment.

It is important to note that CBT for addiction often incorporates traditional CBT techniques, such as identifying and challenging negative thoughts, behavioral activation, and developing coping skills, which are also used in treating depression, anxiety, and OCD. However, the specific cognitive interventions mentioned above differentiate CBT for addiction from CBT for these other mental health issues.

Three CBT Strategies for Addiction Intervention

Cognitive Behavioral Therapy (CBT) offers a range of effective strategies for intervention in addiction. These strategies aim to address the underlying thoughts, emotions, and behaviors that contribute to substance abuse and dependence.

1. Identifying and Challenging Automatic Thoughts

One of the key cognitive interventions for addiction is identifying and challenging automatic thoughts and beliefs related to substance use.

"I can't have fun without using substances."
This belief assumes that substances are necessary for enjoyment or socializing, making it challenging to imagine engaging in these activities without relying on drugs or alcohol.

"Substances help me cope with stress"
This thought suggests that substances are the only effective way to manage stress and difficult emotions, leading to a reliance on substances as a coping mechanism.

"I can control my substance use."
This belief often leads individuals to underestimate their level of dependence or addiction, making it difficult to recognize the need for help or to make positive changes.

"I need substances to feel confident or outgoing."

This thought implies that substances are necessary for boosting self-esteem or overcoming social anxiety, making it challenging to develop healthier coping mechanisms or build genuine self-confidence.

"I deserve to reward myself with substances."

This belief may stem from a sense of entitlement or the idea that substances are a justified indulgence, which can make it difficult to break free from the cycle of substance use.

"Substances make me more creative or productive."

This thought suggests that substances enhance creativity or productivity, making it challenging to believe in one's abilities without their influence and potentially hindering personal growth.

"I can quit anytime I want."

This belief often leads to procrastination and delaying necessary change as individuals convince themselves that they have complete control over their substance use.

"I'm too far gone to recover."

This thought can arise from a sense of hopelessness or previous failed attempts at quitting, making it challenging to believe in the possibility of recovery and seeking help.

"Using substances is the only way to fit in with my peers."

This belief can create a strong desire to conform and be accepted by others who use substances, making it challenging to resist peer pressure and make independent choices.

I'm not as bad as others who use substances."

This thought compares one's own substance use to others who may have more severe issues, potentially minimizing the negative impact of one's own behavior and delaying seeking help when needed.

CBT can help you examine the irrational beliefs that may be fueling your addiction. By replacing these beliefs with healthier and more realistic ones, you can gradually overcome the dependency on substances and develop healthier coping mechanisms.

Replacing Beliefs with More Realistic Ones

'I can't have fun without using substances'	'I can find enjoyment in other activities and connect with people without relying on drugs or alcohol.'
'Substances help me cope with stress'	'There are healthier ways to manage stress, such as exercise, mindfulness, or talking to a therapist.'
'I can control my substance use'	'Recognizing the extent of my dependence allows me to seek help and make positive changes in my life.'
'I need substances to feel confident or outgoing'	'I can build genuine self-confidence and overcome social anxiety through personal growth, self-care, and healthy relationships.'

'I deserve to reward myself with substances'	'I can find healthier ways to reward myself, such as engaging in hobbies, spending time with loved ones, or treating myself to something non-substance related.'
'Substances make me more creative or productive'	'I have the ability to be creative and productive without relying on substances. I can tap into my natural abilities and find inspiration through other means.'
'I can quit anytime I want'	'Recognizing the challenges of quitting, I can seek support and develop a plan to overcome my addiction.'
'I'm too far gone to recover'	'Recovery is possible for anyone, and I have the strength and resources to make positive changes in my life.'
'Using substances is the only way to fit in with my peers'	'I can find meaningful connections and acceptance by surrounding myself with supportive people who share my values and interests.'
'I'm not as bad as others who use substances'	'Comparing myself to others is not helpful. I acknowledge the negative impact of my substance use and take responsibility for my own recovery.'

Through CBT, individuals can challenge and replace these irrational beliefs, allowing them to break free from the cycle of substance use and develop healthier patterns of thinking and behavior.

2. Identifying Triggers and High-risk Situations

To effectively navigate the challenges of addiction recovery, it's crucial for you to identify the specific triggers and high-risk situations that may lead to substance abuse. Identifying triggers is an essential step in your journey towards a happier, healthier life. Triggers can be anything that prompts the urge to use drugs or engage in other addictive behaviors. They can be external, such as certain people, places, or events, or internal, such as emotions, thoughts, or physical sensations.

Once you have identified your triggers, it's important to develop effective coping strategies to deal with them. Emotional regulation is key in this process. Learning to recognize and manage your emotions can help prevent you from turning to substances as a way to cope.

Self-awareness also plays a vital role. By understanding your thoughts, feelings, and behaviors, you can gain insight into the underlying causes of your addiction and develop healthier ways of responding.

To identify the specific triggers and high-risk situations that may lead to substance abuse, follow these actionable steps:

1. **Self-reflection and awareness:** Take some time to reflect on your past substance abuse experiences and identify patterns or situations that have triggered your addictive behavior. Consider the following questions:

a. What emotions or situations tend to precede or accompany substance abuse episodes?
   b. Are there specific people, places, or events that consistently lead to substance abuse?
   c. How do these triggers make you feel?

2. **Keep a trigger journal:** Start a journal to record your daily experiences, emotions, and behaviors related to substance abuse. Note down any situations that you suspect might be triggers. Include details such as the time, location, people involved, and your emotional state before and after the situation.

3. **Seek professional guidance:** Consulting with a therapist, counselor, or addiction specialist can provide valuable insights and support. They can help you identify triggers and high-risk situations more effectively by guiding you through evidence-based techniques and assessments.

4. **Engage in support groups:** Joining a support group or attending addiction recovery meetings can connect you with individuals who have faced similar challenges. Sharing experiences and listening to others can help you gain insight into your own triggers and high-risk situations.

5. **Surround yourself with positive influences:** Evaluate your social circle and identify individuals who may be enabling or encouraging your substance abuse. Consider distancing yourself from these people and seek out positive and supportive relationships that promote sobriety.

6. **Practice mindfulness and self-care:** Develop healthy coping mechanisms and stress management techniques to reduce your vulnerability to triggers. Engaging in activities like meditation, exercise, hobbies, and relaxation techniques can help you stay focused and mindful of your emotions and triggers.

7. **Experiment with avoidance and exposure**: Gradually expose yourself to situations that you suspect may be triggers. Start with less risky situations and practice coping strategies to resist the urge to abuse substances. This can help you build resilience and develop effective strategies to cope with triggers in the long run.

8. **Monitor progress and adjust strategies:** Continuously monitor your progress in identifying and managing triggers. Regularly review your trigger journal and assess which strategies are working well for you. Adjust and refine your approach as needed to ensure ongoing success in overcoming substance abuse.

While Cognitive Behavioral Therapy (CBT) techniques can be helpful for identifying triggers and high-risk situations on your own, there are some potential risks to be aware of:

- Without the guidance of a trained therapist, you may misinterpret or misapply CBT techniques, which could lead to ineffective or potentially harmful outcomes.

- Exploring triggers and high-risk situations can bring up intense emotions. If you are not equipped to handle these emotions or have a support system in place, it could lead to increased distress or exacerbation of symptoms.
- Self-assessment may be biased or lack objectivity, leading to inaccurate identification of triggers or high-risk situations.
- CBT techniques can be complex and require a thorough understanding of underlying principles. Without proper training or supervision, you may not fully grasp the techniques or their potential impact.

To minimize these risks, it is generally recommended to seek guidance from a qualified mental health professional who can provide appropriate support, ensure accurate application, and help address any emotional challenges that may arise.

3. Coping Skills to Prevent Relapse

Developing effective coping skills is essential for preventing relapse and maintaining long-term recovery from addiction. This means finding alternative ways to deal with stress, sadness, or boredom that don't involve addictive substances or behaviors.

There are several coping skills that can be helpful in preventing relapse and maintaining long-term recovery from addiction. Here are some important ones:

1. **Healthy Communication**
   Developing effective communication skills can help individuals express their emotions and needs in a healthy and assertive manner, reducing the likelihood of turning to substances or addictive behaviors as a coping mechanism. This can be achieved through therapy, support groups, or communication workshops.

2. **Stress Management**
   Learning how to manage stress is crucial in preventing relapse. Techniques such as deep breathing exercises, mindfulness meditation, regular physical exercise, and engaging in hobbies or activities that promote relaxation can all be helpful in reducing stress levels.

3. **Building Supportive Relationships**
   Surrounding oneself with a strong support network is vital for recovery. This may include attending support groups and therapy sessions or developing healthy relationships with family and friends who are supportive of the recovery process.

4. **Developing Healthy Coping Mechanisms**
   Finding healthy ways to cope with difficult emotions or situations is crucial. This can involve engaging in activities that bring joy and fulfillment, such as pursuing hobbies, engaging in creative outlets, practicing self-care activities, or participating in support groups where individuals can share their experiences and receive guidance.

5. **Self-Care**

    Taking care of oneself physically, emotionally, and mentally is essential in preventing relapse. This includes getting enough sleep, eating a balanced diet, exercising regularly, practicing relaxation techniques, and engaging in activities that bring joy and fulfillment.

By actively engaging in these steps and consistently practicing healthy coping skills, you can significantly reduce the risk of relapse and maintain long-term recovery from addiction.

Building a Relapse Prevention Plan

How can you effectively create a relapse prevention plan to maintain your sobriety and achieve long-term recovery? Developing coping strategies, identifying warning signs, setting realistic goals, seeking support, and practicing self-care are key elements in creating a relapse prevention plan.

Creating a relapse prevention plan is an ongoing process that requires commitment and self-reflection. By incorporating these strategies into your plan, you can increase your chances of maintaining sobriety and achieving long-term recovery.

Remember, you're capable of rewriting your story and living a fulfilling, substance-free life. Stay strong, stay committed, and know that you aren't alone on this journey.

Personalized Relapse Prevention Plan Worksheet

Congratulations on taking the first step towards maintaining your sobriety! This worksheet will help you create a personalized relapse prevention plan using Cognitive Behavioral Therapy (CBT) techniques. Remember, you've got this, and we're here to support you every step of the way!

Step 1: Identify Triggers
Think about the people, places, emotions, or situations that have triggered your addictive behavior in the past. Write them down below:

1. _____
2. _____
3. _____
4. _____
5. _____

Step 2: Challenge Negative Thoughts
Our thoughts can often lead to relapse. Identify negative thoughts that may arise when facing triggers and challenge them with positive alternatives:

Negative Thought: _____
Positive Alternative: _____

Negative Thought: _____
Positive Alternative: _____

Negative Thought: _____
Positive Alternative: _____

Step 3: Plan for Cravings
Cravings are a normal part of addiction recovery. Create a plan to manage cravings effectively:

Keep a list of distractions: _____
Practice deep breathing exercises: _____
Reach out to your support system: _____
Engage in a physical activity: _____
Write down your reasons for staying sober: _____
Other strategies: _____

Step 4: Self-Care Strategies
Taking care of yourself is crucial for maintaining sobriety. List self-care activities that you enjoy and can turn to when needed:

1. _____
2. _____
3. _____
4. _____
5. _____

Step 5: Building a Support Network

Having a strong support system is essential for recovery. Write down the names of people you can rely on for encouragement and assistance:

1. _____
2. _____
3. _____
4. _____
5. _____

Step 6: Celebrate Milestones

Recognize and celebrate your achievements along the way. Write down rewards or treats you will give yourself for reaching specific milestones:

After 30 days of sobriety: _____
After 90 days of sobriety: _____
After 6 months of sobriety: _____
After 1 year of sobriety: _____

Remember, recovery is a journey, and relapse is not failure. Use this worksheet as a guide to create your personalized relapse prevention plan. Stay motivated, stay positive, and stay committed to your sobriety. You've got this!

Chapter 6
Managing Insomnia with CBT

Insomnia, a common sleep disorder, affects millions of people worldwide. The struggle to fall asleep or stay asleep can have a significant impact on one's physical, mental, and emotional well-being. In recent years, the power of Cognitive Behavioral Therapy (CBT) in addressing insomnia has been recognized, offering hope and effective management strategies for those suffering from this debilitating condition.

This chapter will delve into the effectiveness of CBT as a treatment for insomnia. CBT approaches insomnia as a multifaceted issue, targeting both the cognitive and behavioral aspects that contribute to sleep difficulties.

Understanding the Causes and Impact of Insomnia

The understanding of insomnia and its treatment has evolved throughout history. While ancient civilizations recognized sleep disturbances, it was not until the late 20th century that the power of CBT was discovered. Traditional methods like medication and relaxation techniques provided temporary relief but failed to address the root causes of insomnia. CBT, with its focus on changing negative thought patterns and behaviors, emerged as a breakthrough treatment for insomnia.

There are several potential causes of insomnia, including:

1. **Stress and anxiety:** Emotional or psychological factors such as excessive worrying, tension, or traumatic experiences can make it difficult to fall asleep or stay asleep.

2. **Poor sleep habits:** Irregular sleep schedule, excessive daytime napping, stimulating activities before bedtime, or an uncomfortable sleep environment can disrupt sleep patterns.

3. **Medical conditions:** Conditions like chronic pain, asthma, allergies, gastrointestinal problems, hormonal imbalances (such as thyroid disorders), and neurological conditions (like Parkinson's disease) can interfere with sleep.

4. **Medications:** Certain medications, such as antidepressants, corticosteroids, and medications for asthma or high blood pressure, can disrupt sleep patterns as a side effect.

5. **Substance use/can** cause difficulties fallingThe use of substances like caffeine, nicotine, alcohol, and certain drugs can interfere with sleep quality and contribute to insomnia.

6. **Sleep disorders:** Conditions like sleep apnea, restless leg syndrome, and insomnia disorder itself can cause difficulties in falling asleep or staying asleep.

7. **Environmental factors:** Noise, light, extreme temperatures, or an uncomfortable bed or pillow can make it hard to fall asleep or stay asleep.

8. **Disruptions in the circadian rhythm:** Shift work, jet lag, or frequently changing sleep schedules can disrupt the body's natural sleep-wake cycle.

These are general causes of insomnia, and the specific causes can vary from person to person. If you are experiencing persistent insomnia, consult a healthcare professional for an accurate diagnosis and appropriate treatment.

Insomnia can have far-reaching consequences, affecting various aspects of a person's life. Physically, it can lead to fatigue, a weakened immune system, and an increased risk of accidents. Mentally, it can cause difficulty concentrating, memory problems, and decreased cognitive performance. Emotionally, insomnia often contributes to irritability and mood swings and may even trigger or worsen mental health conditions such as anxiety and depression. Additionally, the impact on social interactions, work productivity, and overall quality of life cannot be overstated.

Having insomnia can be an incredibly challenging and frustrating experience, and I want you to know that you're not alone in this struggle. I understand how difficult it can be to fall asleep or stay asleep night after night, and the toll it can take on your physical and mental well-being.

One of the most distressing aspects of insomnia is the feeling of exhaustion that never seems to go away. You may lay in bed for hours, tossing and turning, desperately trying to find a comfortable position or a peaceful state of mind. Your body longs for rest, but your mind refuses to quiet down. It's as if your thoughts and worries become amplified in the silence of the night, making it nearly impossible to find the tranquility necessary for sleep.

As the nights turn into weeks and then months, the lack of sleep starts to affect your daily life. You may find it difficult to concentrate, make decisions, or perform even simple tasks. Your energy levels plummet, and you feel drained and irritable throughout the day. This constant fatigue can lead to a sense of hopelessness as if you're trapped in a never-ending cycle of sleeplessness.

The frustration of insomnia often manifests in feelings of anxiety and restlessness. As bedtime approaches, there may be a sense of dread, fearing another night of tossing and turning. You may become preoccupied with thoughts of sleep, constantly checking the clock and calculating how many hours you have left before the alarm goes off. This anxiety only exacerbates the problem, making it even harder to relax and fall asleep.

Sleep deprivation also takes a toll on your emotional well-being. The simplest of tasks can become overwhelming, and your emotions may feel heightened and unpredictable. You may experience bouts of sadness, frustration, or irritability, often feeling like a different version of yourself. It's not uncommon to question your own sanity or wonder if you'll ever find relief from this exhausting condition.

I want you to know that I understand the immense impact insomnia can have on your life. It's important to seek support from healthcare professionals who can help you develop strategies to manage your insomnia. Remember, you are not alone, and there is hope for better sleep in the future.

Seven Key CBT Components for Managing Insomnia

Cognitive-behavioral therapy (CBT) is an effective treatment for managing insomnia. It includes several key components:

- Sleep education to provide a comprehensive understanding of sleep.
- Cognitive restructuring to challenge negative thoughts about sleep.
- Sleep hygiene to establish healthy habits.
- Relaxation techniques to promote relaxation.
- Stimulus control to associate the bed with sleep.
- Sleep restriction to increase sleep efficiency.
- Maintenance strategies to sustain healthy sleep patterns.

CBT for insomnia is a comprehensive approach that addresses various aspects of sleep and helps individuals manage their insomnia effectively.

1. Sleep Education

To understand sleep better, it is crucial to familiarize ourselves with the sleep cycle. The sleep cycle consists of four stages: NREM stages 1, 2, 3, and REM sleep. Each stage has unique characteristics, such as brain wave patterns, eye movements, and muscle activity. Throughout the night, the sleep cycle repeats approximately every 90 minutes, with REM sleep becoming longer in subsequent cycles.

Quality sleep provides numerous benefits for our physical, mental, and emotional well-being. In terms of physical health, sleep plays a vital role in restoring and repairing the body's tissues, including the heart and blood vessels. It also boosts the immune system, reducing the risk of illness and chronic diseases. Additionally, sleep regulates hormone production, aiding in weight management and appetite control.

Sleep is also crucial for mental and emotional well-being. It enhances cognitive functions, including memory consolidation, problem-solving, and creativity. Quality sleep improves mood regulation, reducing the risk of depression, anxiety, and emotional instability. Moreover, it supports optimal brain development in children and adolescents.

Fortunately, Cognitive Behavioral Therapy (CBT) offers effective techniques for managing insomnia. By addressing the underlying causes of your sleep disturbance and implementing strategies to improve your sleep hygiene, CBT can help you break free from the grip of insomnia.

2. Cognitive Restructuring for Sleep-related Thoughts

Change the way you think about sleep with cognitive restructuring techniques. If you find yourself struggling with sleep-related thoughts that contribute to poor sleep quality, cognitive restructuring can help.

Cognitive restructuring is a powerful tool that can help you identify and change thought patterns that are negatively impacting your sleep. By challenging and replacing these thoughts, you can alleviate sleep-related anxiety and improve your overall sleep experience.

When it comes to sleep, our thoughts play a significant role in determining the quality of our rest. Negative thoughts and worries about sleep can create a cycle of anxiety that perpetuates sleep problems. Cognitive restructuring aims to interrupt this cycle.

To begin the process of cognitive restructuring for better sleep, it's important to become aware of your sleep-related thoughts. Pay attention to the specific thoughts that arise when you think about sleep or when you're lying in bed trying to fall asleep. Here are some common sleep-related thoughts that may need to be restructured, along with examples of how to reframe them:

Negative Thought	Restructured Thought
"I'll never be able to fall asleep tonight."	"It's normal to have difficulty falling asleep sometimes, but I can practice relaxation techniques to help me drift off."
"I always have terrible sleep."	"I've had challenging nights in the past, but I can make changes to improve my sleep quality and create a better bedtime routine."
"If I don't get enough sleep, tomorrow will be a disaster."	"While sleep is important, I can still function and handle any challenges that come my way even if I had a less-than-perfect night of sleep."
"I'm so anxious about not being able to fall asleep."	"It's normal to feel some anxiety about sleep, but I can use relaxation techniques and positive thinking to calm my mind and prepare for sleep."
"My mind is always racing at night, I'll never be able to quiet it down."	"It may take some practice, but I can develop strategies like mindfulness or deep breathing to help calm my mind and create a more peaceful sleep environment."

| "I need a perfect eight hours of sleep or I won't function well." | "While aiming for a solid amount of sleep is important, even a shorter or interrupted night of sleep can still leave me feeling rested and capable." |

Remember to choose restructured thoughts that resonate with you personally and feel inspired for a better night's sleep. Start rewiring your mind today for better sleep and enjoy the benefits of a more peaceful and restorative rest.

The Power of Yet

One sleep coaching tip that incorporates cognitive reframing in Cognitive Behavioral Therapy (CBT) is called *"The Power of Yet."* This technique involves reframing negative thoughts about sleep and replacing them with more positive and empowering statements.

When struggling with sleep, many individuals may have thoughts like *"I'll never be able to fall asleep"* or *"I always have trouble sleeping."* These thoughts can create anxiety and make it even harder to fall asleep. However, using the power of yet, you can reframe these thoughts by adding the word *"yet"* at the end.

For example, instead of saying *"I'll never be able to fall asleep,"* you can reframe it as *"I haven't been able to fall asleep easily yet."* By adding *"yet,"* you acknowledge that while it may be difficult at the moment, it doesn't mean it will always be that way.

This reframing technique helps shift the focus from a fixed mindset to a growth mindset. It reminds you that your current sleep difficulties are temporary and changeable. By adopting a growth mindset, you open yourself up to possibilities and potential solutions, which can reduce anxiety and improve sleep quality.

Remember, the power of yet is not a magical solution, but it can be a helpful tool to reframe negative thoughts and cultivate a more positive and hopeful outlook toward sleep.

3. Sleep Hygiene to Establish Healthy Routines

Sleep hygiene refers to a set of practices and routines that promote healthy and restful sleep. It is an important component of Cognitive Behavioral Therapy (CBT) for sleep disorders. By following these practices, individuals can establish healthy sleep habits and improve the quality and duration of their sleep. Here are some effective ways to implement sleep hygiene techniques on your own:

- **Stick to a Regular Sleep Schedule**
  Go to bed and wake up at the same time every day, even on weekends. This helps regulate your body's internal clock and promotes a consistent sleep-wake cycle.

- **Create a Soothing Bedtime Routine**
  Establish a relaxing routine before bed to signal to your body that it's time to sleep. This could include activities like reading, taking a warm bath, practicing relaxation exercises, or listening to calming music.

- **Create a Sleep-friendly Environment**
  Make sure your bedroom is conducive to sleep. Keep the room cool, dark, and quiet. Use comfortable bedding and a supportive mattress. Consider using earplugs, eye masks, or white noise machines if necessary.

- **Limit Exposure to Electronics**
  Avoid using electronic devices such as smartphones, tablets, or laptops close to bedtime. The blue light emitted by these devices can interfere with your sleep by suppressing the production of melatonin, a hormone that regulates sleep.

- **Avoid Stimulants and Heavy Meals**
  Limit your consumption of caffeine, nicotine, and alcohol, especially close to bedtime. These substances can disrupt your sleep patterns and make it harder to fall asleep or stay asleep. Additionally, avoid heavy meals or excessive fluid intake before bed to prevent discomfort or disruptions during the night.

- **Exercise Regularly**
  Engage in regular physical activity during the day, but avoid exercising too close to bedtime. Exercise can help promote better sleep, but doing it too late in the evening may increase alertness and make it difficult to fall asleep.

- **Manage Stress**
  Practice stress management techniques such as mindfulness, deep breathing, or journaling to help relax your mind

before bed. If you find yourself worrying or experiencing racing thoughts at night, try setting aside designated *"worry time"* earlier in the day to address these concerns.

- **Limit Napping**
  If you have trouble sleeping at night, limit daytime napping to ensure you're tired enough to fall asleep at the desired bedtime. If you do nap, keep it short (around 20 to 30 minutes) and avoid napping too close to bedtime.

- **Associate Your Bed with Sleep**
  Reserve your bed for sleep and intimacy only. Avoid using your bed for work, watching TV, or other stimulating activities. By associating your bed solely with sleep, you can train your brain to recognize it as a space for rest.

- **Seek Professional Help if Needed**
  If you continue to struggle with sleep despite practicing good sleep hygiene, consider seeking help from a healthcare professional or a therapist specializing in sleep disorders. They can provide further guidance and support.

Remember, it may take time for your body to adjust to these changes, so be patient and persistent in your efforts.

4. Relaxation and Mindfulness Techniques for Better Sleep

Improve your sleep quality by practicing relaxation and mindfulness techniques. Getting a good night's sleep is essential for your overall well-being, and incorporating these techniques into your bedtime routine can help you achieve a state of deep relaxation and inner calm.

This guide offers a collection of simple and doable routines that utilize Cognitive Behavioral Therapy (CBT) techniques to promote relaxation and calmness before sleep. Follow these easy instructions to find the routine that works best for you.

Deep Breathing:

1. Find a comfortable position in bed.
2. Inhale deeply through your nose, filling your lungs with air.
3. Hold your breath for a few seconds, allowing the relaxation to set in.
4. Exhale slowly through your mouth, releasing any tension or stress.
5. Repeat this deep breathing pattern for a few minutes, focusing solely on your breath. Feel the sense of calmness wash over you.

Progressive Muscle Relaxation:

1. Begin by tensing the muscles in your toes and feet as tightly as you can.

2. Hold the tension for a few seconds, then release and feel the relaxation spread through your lower body.
3. Gradually work your way up, tensing and releasing each muscle group, including calves, thighs, abdomen, chest, shoulders, arms, and face.
4. Take your time with each muscle group, allowing yourself to fully let go of any tension.
5. As you progress, visualize the tension melting away and a deep sense of relaxation taking over your entire body.

Guided Imagery:

1. Close your eyes and imagine yourself in a peaceful and serene environment, such as a beach or a forest.
2. Engage your senses by visualizing every detail: the sound of waves crashing, the gentle breeze on your skin, or the scent of flowers.
3. Immerse yourself in this imaginary world, allowing the soothing sensations to wash away any worries or racing thoughts.
4. Stay in this state of tranquility for a few minutes, enjoying the calmness it brings.

Sleep Meditation:

1. Find a comfortable position in bed, ensuring your body is fully supported.
2. Focus your attention on your breath, noticing the sensation of each inhale and exhale.
3. As thoughts arise, acknowledge them without judgment and let them pass by like clouds in the sky.

4. Gently redirect your attention back to your breath, using it as an anchor to stay present in the moment.
5. Continue this practice, allowing your mind to settle and your body to relax, preparing you for a restful night's sleep.

Incorporating these relaxation and mindfulness routines into your bedtime routine can significantly improve your sleep quality. Remember, consistency is key, so try to practice these techniques regularly. With time and practice, you'll develop a healthy sleep routine and find relief from insomnia. Sleep well!

5. Establishing a Bed-Sleep Association for Better Sleep Quality

Tailor your routine to activities that you find particularly relaxing and enjoyable. This makes it more likely that you'll stick to the routine and look forward to it each night.

Creating a calming sleep environment
- Experiment with aromatherapy by using lavender essential oils or other scents that promote relaxation.
- Consider using soft lighting or a Himalayan salt lamp to create a soothing ambiance.

Utilizing visual cues
- Place visual reminders around your bedroom that associate the space with sleep. This could be a sleep-related quote or a picture of a serene sleep environment.
- These visual cues can help reinforce the idea of the bed being a place for rest.

Using guided imagery or visualization
- Before bed, imagine yourself in a peaceful and comfortable sleep environment. Visualize yourself falling asleep easily and waking up refreshed.
- This technique can help reduce anxiety and create positive associations with sleep.

Guided Visualization Exercise

Find a quiet and comfortable place where you can relax and lie down. Close your eyes and begin taking slow, deep breaths. Let the tension in your body melt away with each exhale.

Imagine yourself in a serene and magical forest. Picture tall, ancient trees surrounding you, their branches swaying gently in the breeze. It's a warm, peaceful evening, and the soft golden light of the setting sun filters through the leaves.

As you walk deeper into the forest, you come across a cozy, inviting cottage nestled amidst a clearing. You approach the cottage and notice a warm glow emanating from its windows. This is your special sleep sanctuary.

As you enter, you find yourself in a beautifully decorated bedroom. The bed is adorned with soft, luxurious linens and fluffy pillows. Take a moment to notice the soothing colors and textures of the room, as they promote relaxation and tranquility.

Sit on the edge of the bed and feel its comforting support beneath you. Focus on the sensation of the soft mattress cradling your body. Take a few moments to appreciate the comfort and safety of this space.

Now, imagine a gentle, melodic lullaby playing softly in the background. Allow the soothing melody to wash over you, further relaxing your mind and body. With each note, feel yourself becoming more and more ready for a restful sleep.

Lie down on the bed and allow yourself to sink into its plushness. Feel the weight of your body being fully supported by the mattress. As you settle in, notice how your muscles release any remaining tension, as if they are being gently caressed by the bed.

Now, imagine a soft, warm light enveloping your body. This light represents the peaceful energy of sleep. Feel it wrapping around you, creating a cocoon of tranquility. Allow yourself to surrender to this gentle embrace of sleep.

As you drift off into sleep, imagine vivid scenes of tranquility and serenity. Picture yourself floating on a calm lake, feeling weightless and free. Imagine being surrounded by a soft, comforting mist that carries away any worries or stress. Visualize yourself in a peaceful meadow, lying on a blanket of soft grass, gazing up at a clear, starlit sky.

> *As you continue to visualize these serene scenes, allow your mind to become still and quiet. Let go of any thoughts or concerns that may be lingering. Trust that this peaceful imagery will help you drift into a deep and rejuvenating sleep.*
>
> Take a few moments to bask in this feeling of tranquility and contentment. When you are ready, slowly bring your awareness back to your physical surroundings. Wiggle your fingers and toes, and gently open your eyes.

You can revisit this guided visualization practice whenever you need to relax and associate bed and sleep with a sense of peace and calm.

Remember, consistency is key when using stimulus control techniques. Stick to the routine and make adjustments as needed, but try to maintain a regular sleep schedule and bedtime routine to reinforce the association between bed and sleep.

6. Enhancing Sleep Efficiency through Sleep Restriction

Sleep restriction is a technique commonly used in cognitive-behavioral therapy for insomnia (CBT-I) to enhance sleep efficiency. It involves limiting the time spent in bed to match the actual sleep time, thereby increasing sleep drive and promoting more consolidated and restful sleep. While it is typically performed under the guidance of a trained therapist, there are ways in which individuals can effectively perform sleep restriction by themselves.

Here are some steps to effectively implement sleep restriction in CBT-I:

Step 1. Establish a consistent wake-up time.
Determine the time you need to wake up each day and stick to it, even on weekends. This helps regulate your body's internal clock and create a consistent sleep schedule.

Step 2. Keep a sleep diary.
Before starting sleep restriction, keep a sleep diary for a week or two. Record the time you go to bed, the time you try to fall asleep, the time you wake up, and any awakenings during the night. This will help identify your actual sleep time.

Step 3. Calculate your sleep efficiency.
Sleep efficiency is the ratio of time spent asleep to time spent in bed. To calculate your sleep efficiency, divide the total time asleep by the total time spent in bed and multiply by 100. For example, if you spend 8 hours in bed but only sleep for 6 hours, your sleep efficiency is 75%.

4. Set a consistent bedtime based on sleep efficiency.
Determine the amount of time you are actually sleeping in bed by subtracting the time you spend awake from your total time in bed. For example, if you spend 8 hours in bed but only sleep for 6 hours, your actual sleep time is 6 hours. Set your bedtime based on this actual sleep time.

Step 5. Gradually adjust bedtime.

Start by setting your bedtime to the actual sleep time calculated in step 4. If you find that you are falling asleep quickly and sleeping well for at least 85% of the time spent in bed, you can gradually increase your bedtime by 15-30 minutes every few nights.

To build up sleep drive, avoid napping during the day. If you feel the need to nap, try to limit it to a brief power nap of no more than 20 minutes.

Step 6. Monitor progress.

Keep track of your sleep efficiency and how you feel during the day. If you notice improvements in sleep quality and daytime functioning, continue gradually adjusting your bedtime. If your sleep efficiency decreases or you experience increased daytime sleepiness, consult with a healthcare professional or sleep specialist.

Implementing sleep restrictions can initially lead to some temporary sleep deprivation and increased fatigue. However, over time, it can help consolidate sleep and improve sleep efficiency.

While self-implementing sleep restriction can be effective for some individuals, it is always recommended to seek guidance from a trained therapist or healthcare professional experienced in CBT-I, especially if you have complex sleep issues or underlying medical conditions. They can provide personalized guidance and support throughout the process.

7. Sustaining Healthy Sleep Patterns with Maintenance Strategies

In addition to the commonly mentioned strategies for maintaining a good sleeping pattern, such as establishing a consistent sleep schedule and creating a relaxing bedtime routine, there are a few other techniques you can incorporate into your routine. These will help you achieve better sleep quality and ensure a restful night's sleep. Here are some additional maintenance strategies you can try:

- **Use a Weighted Blanket**
  Weighted blankets have been shown to reduce anxiety and promote relaxation, leading to improved sleep quality. They provide a gentle, calming pressure that can help you feel more secure and comfortable in bed.

- **Try Aromatherapy**
  Certain scents, like lavender, have been found to have a calming effect and promote sleep. Consider using essential oils or a lavender-scented pillow spray to create a soothing atmosphere in your bedroom.

- **Invest in a High-Quality Mattress and Pillows**
  The right mattress and pillows can make a significant difference in your sleep quality. Choose ones that provide proper support and comfort, tailored to your individual needs.

- **Use Sleep-Tracking Apps or Devices**
  There are various smartphone apps and wearable devices that can help you track your sleep patterns and provide insights into your sleep quality. These tools can help you identify any patterns or issues that may be affecting your sleep.

In some cases, doctors may prescribe short-term use of sleep medications to help with insomnia. However, these should only be used under professional guidance, as they carry potential risks and side effects.

Remember, what works for one person may not work for another, so it's essential to find an approach that suits your individual needs.

Sleep is not just a necessity; it is a gift that we can cherish every night. By adopting a Cognitive Behavioral Therapy (CBT) approach towards sleep, we can transform our mindset and cultivate a positive relationship with the act of slumber.

Rather than viewing sleep as a mere interruption to our daily lives, let us embrace it as a vital component of our well-being. Recognize that sleep is not a luxury but a fundamental need that rejuvenates our body and mind. Challenge any negative thoughts or anxieties about sleep by replacing them with positive affirmations and realistic expectations.

Shift your focus from the fear of sleeplessness to the anticipation of restful nights. Cultivate a bedtime routine that promotes relaxation and signals to your body and mind that it's time to unwind.

Engage in activities that calm your thoughts and create a serene environment conducive to sleep.

Remember, sleep is not a battle to be won or lost; it is a peaceful surrender to the healing power of rest. Embrace the quiet stillness of the night and allow yourself to be embraced by its gentle embrace. Trust in the natural rhythm of your body to guide you towards the restorative sleep you deserve.

In the end, sleep is not just a necessity; it is a sanctuary where we find solace, renewal, and the opportunity to awaken to a brighter tomorrow.

Chapter 7
Ways to Cope with Stress Using CBT

In this chapter, we will explore effective techniques for coping with stress using Cognitive Behavioral Therapy (CBT). Stress can damage our physical and mental health, as well as our relationships. By incorporating stress reduction techniques into our daily lives, we can improve our overall well-being and quality of life.

Chronic stress can lead to health problems such as high blood pressure, heart disease, weakened immunity, and digestive issues. Engaging in stress reduction techniques can help lower our body's stress response and reduce the risk of these conditions. It can also alleviate mental health issues like anxiety, depression, and difficulties with concentration.

Excessive stress can cause emotional imbalances, leading to irritability, anger, and emotional exhaustion. Stress reduction techniques can help us regulate our emotions, find inner calm, and improve our emotional stability. These techniques can also improve our sleep quality, which in turn boosts our energy levels, mood, and cognitive function.

Stress can impair our focus, decision-making, and productivity. By utilizing stress reduction techniques, we can minimize mental distractions, increase our focus, and enhance our productivity. This, in turn, improves our work performance and effectiveness in daily activities.

Furthermore, chronic stress can strain relationships and hinder social interactions. Stress reduction techniques can improve emotional well-being, make us more present and empathetic in our relationships, and foster better communication and healthier connections with others.

Stress reduction techniques are crucial for promoting physical health, mental well-being, emotional stability, sleep quality, productivity, and healthy relationships. By implementing these techniques, we can enhance our overall quality of life, find balance, and cultivate a sense of well-being.

If you find yourself struggling with stress, CBT offers a valuable set of coping strategies to navigate through stressful situations with resilience and ease. Remember, you are not alone, and there are effective ways to manage and reduce stress.

Understanding the Nature of Stress

Stress is a natural part of life, but it's essential to recognize its causes, impact, and effects on your health. Causes of stress can vary from person to person. It could be related to work, relationships, financial issues, or even daily hassles.

Several common signs of stress are relatively easy to recognize. These include:

1. **Physical symptoms:** Headaches, muscle tension or pain, fatigue, sleep disturbances, upset stomach, and changes in appetite.

2. **Emotional symptoms:** Feeling overwhelmed, irritable, anxious, or restless. Mood swings, increased irritability, and difficulty relaxing or quieting the mind.

3. **Cognitive symptoms:** Forgetfulness, difficulty concentrating or making decisions, racing thoughts, constant worrying, and negative thinking.

4. **Behavioral symptoms:** Changes in appetite or sleep patterns, increased use of substances (such as alcohol or drugs), withdrawal from social activities, procrastination or neglecting responsibilities, and increased aggression or irritability.

5. **Interpersonal symptoms:** Relationship problems, increased conflicts or arguments with others, isolation or withdrawal from social activities, and difficulty expressing emotions or feeling misunderstood.

While these signs may indicate stress, they can also be indicative of other underlying issues. If you or someone you know is experiencing persistent or severe symptoms, it is recommended to seek professional help from a healthcare provider or mental health professional.

Identifying Stress Triggers in CBT

Identifying the specific triggers that lead to stress in your life is the first step towards managing it effectively. Once you understand the underlying causes, you can begin to take control of your stress levels.

Identifying Stress Triggers Worksheet

Use the following worksheet to help identify stress triggers in Cognitive Behavioral Therapy (CBT). By completing this worksheet, you will gain insight into the specific situations, thoughts, or events that tend to trigger stress in your life. This awareness will enable you to develop effective strategies to manage and cope with these stressors.

1. Describe the Situation:
Think of a recent or recurring situation in which you experienced stress. Describe it briefly below.

Situation: _____

2. Identify Your Thoughts:
What were the thoughts or beliefs that went through your mind during this situation? Write them down.

Thoughts/beliefs: _____

3. Rate Your Emotional Response:

On a scale of 1 to 10, rate the intensity of your emotional response during this situation, with 1 being minimal and 10 being extreme.

Emotional response rating: _____

4. Physical Sensations:

List any physical sensations or changes you experienced in your body during this situation.

Physical sensations: _____

5. Identify Your Behavioral Responses:

How did you behave or react in response to this situation? List any actions or behaviors that occurred.

Behavioral responses: _____

6. Evaluate the Outcome:

Reflect on the outcome of this situation. Did your response to the stressor help or worsen the situation? Explain briefly.

Outcome evaluation: _____

7. Identify Possible Triggers:

Analyze the information you have gathered so far and identify any patterns or common elements among the situations where you experience stress. These patterns will help you identify your stress triggers.

Possible stress triggers: _____

You can use this same thought process in this worksheet whenever you encounter stressful situations. With practice, you'll learn to approach challenging circumstances by gathering the necessary information to find solutions rather than reacting negatively or responding to stress.

Challenging Stress-inducing Thoughts

Once the triggers have been identified, you can then apply Cognitive Behavioral Therapy (CBT) techniques to challenge thoughts that induce stress. By using CBT techniques, you can effectively manage and overcome stressful thoughts.

To apply Cognitive Behavioral Therapy (CBT) techniques to challenge stress-inducing thoughts, you can follow these steps:

Step 1. Identify the stress-inducing thought.
The first step is to become aware of the specific thought or belief that is causing stress. This could be a negative thought about oneself, a fear, or a catastrophic prediction.

Here are some common examples of stress-inducing thoughts:

- *"I have so much work to do. I'll never get it all done."*
- *"I don't think I can handle this level of responsibility."*
- *"I'm not good enough or smart enough to succeed."*
- *"I always make mistakes; nothing ever goes right for me."*
- *"I'm constantly comparing myself to others and feeling inadequate."*
- *"I can't handle this conflict. It's too overwhelming."*

- *"I'm worried about what others think of me. I need to please everyone."*
- *"I never have enough time to do everything I need to do."*
- *"I'm always under financial pressure. I'll never get out of debt."*
- *"I'm afraid of change and uncertainty; it makes me anxious."*
- *"I'm not good at saying no, so I always take on too much."*
- *"I'm afraid of the future, what if things don't work out?"*
- *"I'm constantly worried about the health and well-being of my loved ones."*
- *"I'm overwhelmed by the constant demands and expectations of others."*
- *"I'm afraid of failure, so I avoid taking risks."*
- *"I'm constantly worried about making the wrong decision."*
- *"I'm always on edge, waiting for something bad to happen."*
- *"I'm afraid of rejection and being judged by others."*

Step 2. Categorize the thought.
Determine if the thought falls into a specific cognitive distortion category. This will help in understanding the nature of the thought and how it may be distorting reality.

These were already discussed in the earlier chapter, but for your reference, here are the cognitive distortions you can use to categorize your stress-inducing thoughts:

- **All-or-Nothing Thinking:** Seeing things as black or white, with no middle ground or shades of gray.
- **Overgeneralization:** Making broad, sweeping conclusions based on a single event or piece of evidence.

- **Mental Filtering:** Focusing solely on the negative aspects of a situation while ignoring any positive aspects.
- **Disqualifying the Positive:** Discounting or dismissing positive experiences or qualities as if they don't count.
- **Jumping to Conclusions:** Making assumptions or reaching conclusions without sufficient evidence.
- **Magnification and Minimization:** Exaggerating the importance of negative events or minimizing the importance of positive events.
- **Emotional Reasoning:** Believing that your emotions reflect the objective reality of a situation without considering other evidence.
- **Personalization:** Taking personal responsibility or blame for events or situations that are outside of your control.
- **Should Statements:** Using words like *"should," "must,"* or *"ought to"* to impose unrealistic expectations on yourself or others.
- **Labeling:** Assigning global, negative labels to oneself or others based on specific behaviors or situations.
- **Catastrophizing:** Expecting the worst-case scenario to happen and exaggerating the potential negative consequences.
- **Mind Reading:** Assuming you know what others are thinking or feeling without any evidence to support it.

This list is not exhaustive, and individuals may experience other cognitive distortions not mentioned here.

Step 3. Gather evidence.
Collect evidence that supports or refutes the stress-inducing thought. Look for objective evidence, alternative explanations, or previous experiences that challenge the validity of the thought.

Step 4. Examine the consequences.
Analyze the impact of holding onto the stress-inducing thought. Consider how it affects emotions, behaviors, and overall well-being. This step helps in realizing the importance of challenging and changing the thought.

Step 5. Generate alternative thoughts.
Come up with alternative, more rational, and balanced thoughts that counteract the stress-inducing thought. These alternative thoughts should be based on the evidence gathered in step 3 and should be more realistic and helpful.

Step 6. Test the alternative thoughts.
Actively test the alternative thoughts by observing how they affect emotions and behaviors. Pay attention to any changes in stress levels or overall well-being. This step helps in reinforcing the effectiveness of the alternative thoughts.

Step 7. Practice thought replacement.
Continuously replace stress-inducing thoughts with the alternative thoughts identified in step 5. Consistent practice is essential for long-term change and resolution of stress.

Step 8. Seek support if needed.
If challenging, stress-inducing thoughts become overwhelming or if progress is slow, it may be helpful to seek support from a therapist or counselor who specializes in CBT. They can provide guidance, feedback, and additional techniques to address the specific stressors.

By following these steps, the reader can effectively analyze stress-inducing thoughts and arrive at a solution or long-term resolution. The process involves gaining awareness of the thought, examining its accuracy and consequences, and then actively challenging and replacing it with more adaptive thoughts. Regular practice and seeking support when necessary can greatly contribute to reducing stress and improving overall well-being.

Relaxation Techniques to Reduce Stress

Breathing exercises, progressive muscle relaxation, mindfulness, and guided visualization are commonly used techniques to reduce stress and induce relaxation.

In addition to these techniques, there are more ingenious ways to reduce stress and induce relaxation that incorporate the concepts of Cognitive Behavioral Therapy (CBT). CBT focuses on identifying and challenging negative thought patterns and replacing them with more positive and realistic ones. Here are a few examples:

- **Gratitude exercises:** Practice gratitude by regularly noting down three things you are grateful for each day. This helps shift focus towards positive aspects of life and promotes a more optimistic mindset.

- **Problem-solving techniques:** Instead of getting overwhelmed by stressors, break them down into smaller, manageable steps and devise a plan to tackle them one at a time. This approach helps reduce stress by providing a sense of control and achievement.

- **Activity scheduling:** Engage in pleasurable and relaxing activities regularly, such as hobbies, exercise, or spending time with loved ones. Prioritizing self-care and enjoyable activities helps counterbalance stress and promotes relaxation.

- **Time Management:** Poor time management can lead to feelings of overwhelm and stress. Utilize strategies such as prioritizing tasks, setting realistic goals, and delegating responsibilities to better manage your time and reduce stress.

- **Assertiveness Training:** Learning to communicate your needs effectively can reduce stress caused by feeling overwhelmed or taken advantage of. Practice assertiveness skills to express your boundaries and needs assertively and respectfully.

- **Humor and Laughter:** Incorporating humor and laughter into your life can be a powerful stress-relief tool. Engage in activities that make you laugh, watch a funny movie, or spend time with people who bring joy and humor to your life.

- **Social Support:** Building and maintaining a strong support network can provide emotional support, perspective, and practical assistance during stressful times. Reach out to friends, family, or support groups for guidance and understanding.

Incorporating these techniques into your stress reduction and relaxation practices can provide a more comprehensive approach to managing stress and promoting overall well-being.

Stress reduction techniques and CBT-based strategies are highly personalized, and it may take some trial and error to find what works best for you.

Thought-Stopping Technique for Stress Management

The Stopping Technique is a simple mindfulness practice that can be used for stress management. It involves taking a pause and consciously redirecting your attention away from stress-inducing thoughts and emotions. Here's how you can effectively do this technique for stress:

1. **Find a quiet and comfortable place.**
   Choose a location where you can sit or stand comfortably without distractions.

2. **Take a deep breath.**
   Begin by taking a deep breath through your nose, filling your lungs, and then exhaling slowly through your mouth. This can help to relax your body and prepare you for the practice.

3. **Acknowledge the stress.**
   Recognize and acknowledge the presence of stress in your mind and body. Allow yourself to fully feel and accept it without judgment.

4. **Say "Stop" internally.**
   In your mind, say the word *"stop"* to yourself. This serves as a mental signal to interrupt the cycle of stressful thoughts and bring your attention back to the present moment.

5. **Observe your surroundings.**
   Shift your focus to the present moment by observing your surroundings. Notice the details of your environment—the sights, sounds, and sensations around you. Grounding yourself in the present can help break the cycle of stress.

6. **Focus on your breath.**
   Direct your attention to your breath. Feel the sensation of the breath entering and leaving your body. Use your breath as an anchor to keep your attention in the present moment.

7. **Practice self-compassion.**
   While you're doing this technique, be kind and compassionate towards yourself. Remind yourself that it's normal to experience stress, and you're taking steps to manage it effectively.

8. **Repeat as needed.**
   If stress arises again, repeat the process by saying *"stop"* mentally, observing your surroundings, and focusing on your breath. Use this technique whenever you feel overwhelmed or need a break from stress.

Stopping Technique is a skill that improves with practice. The more you incorporate it into your daily routine, the better you'll become at managing stress effectively.

Behavioral Activation for Stress

Behavioral Activation (BA) is a therapeutic technique that aims to increase engagement in activities that are rewarding and meaningful, to improve mood and reduce stress. It is based on the belief that the way we behave directly impacts how we feel.

To effectively use BA for stress, here are some simple steps:

1. **Identify activities.**
   Make a list of activities that you enjoy or used to enjoy but have stopped doing due to stress. These can be hobbies, social activities, physical exercise, or self-care activities.

2. **Prioritize activities.**
   Rank the activities based on their importance and how much they contribute to reducing stress. Choose a few activities that are easily accessible and realistic to engage in regularly.

3. **Set goals.**
   Set achievable goals to engage in these activities. Start small with specific and realistic goals. For example, if physical exercise is on your list, you can start with a 15-minute walk three times a week.

4. **Plan and schedule.**
   Create a schedule to incorporate these activities into your daily or weekly routine. Set aside specific time slots for each activity and commit to sticking to the schedule.

5. **Monitor progress.**
   Keep track of your engagement in these activities and how they affect your stress levels. Use a journal or a mood tracker to record your experiences.

6. **Monitor thoughts.**
   Pay attention to any negative thoughts or beliefs that may be hindering your engagement in these activities. Challenge and reframe these thoughts to promote positive behavior.

7. **Seek support.**
   Engage in activities with others if possible, as social support can enhance the benefits of BA. Consider involving friends, and family, or joining groups or clubs related to your chosen activities.

8. **Practice self-care.**
   Alongside engaging in rewarding activities, focus on self-care. Ensure you prioritize rest, relaxation, healthy eating, and good sleep hygiene to support your overall well-being and stress management.

> **TIP:**
> One tip for behavioral activation is to incorporate sensory elements into your activities. Engaging your senses can enhance the overall experience and make it more enjoyable. For example, if you're going for a walk, pay attention to the sounds of nature, feel the texture of different surfaces under your feet, or focus on the smell of flowers or fresh air. By immersing yourself in the sensory details of an activity, you can increase your present moment awareness and amplify the positive impact of behavioral activation on your mood and overall well-being.

Stress doesn't actually stem from the events in your life, but rather from your thoughts and perceptions about those events. If you're able to change your thoughts, you can ultimately change your entire world.

"In the midst of chaos, there is also opportunity." - Sun Tzu

These words from Sun Tzu remind us that even in the most stressful and challenging situations, there are hidden opportunities for growth and success. Embrace the chaos, stay focused on your goals, and adapt to the circumstances. You have the power to transform stress into motivation and achieve greatness.

Chapter 8
Overcoming Procrastination with CBT

Procrastination, is the bane of productivity that afflicts countless individuals, causing unnecessary stress and missed opportunities. The nagging feeling of impending deadlines, the weight of unfinished tasks piling up, and the constant battle between intentions and actions. We all know this struggle too well.

But fear not, for Cognitive Behavioral Therapy (CBT) offers a beacon of hope in the darkness of procrastination. By delving into the underlying thoughts and emotions that drive our avoidance behaviors, CBT equips us with powerful tools to challenge and conquer our procrastination demons.

So, if you're tired of feeling trapped by the clutches of procrastination, join us on this transformative journey towards reclaiming your time and achieving your goals.

Understanding the Underlying Causes of Procrastination

Understanding the root causes of procrastination can help you break free from this habit and achieve greater productivity and fulfillment in your life. Procrastination is a common struggle that affects many individuals, causing frustration and hindering progress. By diving deeper into the underlying causes, we can gain valuable insights that will empower us to overcome procrastination and live a more fulfilling life.

Various factors contribute to procrastination. Psychological factors, such as fear of failure or perfectionism, can paralyze us and prevent us from taking action. When we're afraid of not meeting expectations or making mistakes, we tend to delay tasks to avoid any potential negative outcomes.

Additionally, a lack of clear goals or a sense of purpose can contribute to procrastination. Without a clear direction or motivation, it becomes easier to put things off and prioritize short-term gratification over long-term goals.

The effects of procrastination can be detrimental to our well-being and overall success. It can lead to increased stress levels, decreased self-esteem, and a sense of overwhelm as tasks continue to pile up. Procrastination also robs us of the opportunity to fully engage in the present moment and experience the satisfaction that comes from completing tasks in a timely manner.

Fortunately, there are strategies for combating procrastination and reclaiming control over our lives. Understanding the underlying causes of procrastination is the first step toward overcoming it. By addressing the psychological factors and implementing practical strategies, you can break free from the cycle of procrastination and experience greater productivity, fulfillment, and inner peace in your life. Remember, you have the power to transform your habits and create the life you desire.

Cognitive Restructuring to Overcome Procrastination

Cognitive restructuring is a technique that helps individuals overcome procrastination by challenging and changing their negative thought patterns and beliefs. This approach is effective because procrastination often stems from distorted thinking patterns such as perfectionism, fear of failure, or feeling overwhelmed. By engaging in cognitive restructuring, individuals can reframe their thoughts and develop a more constructive mindset, which in turn helps them overcome procrastination.

Below is a simple worksheet to guide you through the process of cognitive restructuring to overcome procrastination:

1. **Identify the negative thought.**
   Start by recognizing the negative thought or belief that contributes to your procrastination. Write it down in detail.

2. **Challenge the negative thought.**
   Ask yourself if there is evidence to support this thought. Is it based on facts or assumptions? Write down any evidence against this negative thought.

3. **Replace with a realistic thought.**
   Generate a more realistic and positive thought that counteracts the negative belief. For example, if the negative thought is *"I'll never be able to complete this task on time,"* replace it with *"I have successfully completed similar tasks in the past, and I can break this one down into smaller, manageable steps."*

4. **Write down the benefits.**
   List the potential benefits of completing the task or overcoming procrastination. Focus on the positive outcomes that motivate you.

5. **Create an action plan.**
   Break down the task into smaller, achievable steps. Write down a specific plan with deadlines for each step, ensuring it is realistic and manageable.

6. **Seek support.**
   Reach out to someone who can provide encouragement and accountability. Share your action plan with them, and ask for their support in staying on track.

The process I'm about to explain is fairly simple, but it does require practice to be effective. This technique is commonly used in cognitive-behavioral therapy (CBT), but for it to work, it needs to be tailored specifically to address procrastination.

One significant factor contributing to procrastination is the presence or absence of motivation. Additionally, the formation of routines and the adoption of healthy practices are also crucial. These specific elements are the main focus of therapy.

Behavioral Techniques to Increase Motivation and Productivity

When it comes to addressing procrastination, it is important to know some useful techniques that can help if you are struggling with it, even if you already have some knowledge about it. Incorporating these techniques into your routines is key to gradually eliminating procrastination from your system.

Implementation Intentions

This technique involves setting specific plans on when, where, and how you will complete a task. By specifying these details, you create a clear roadmap for yourself, making it easier to follow through with your intentions. To use implementation intentions, follow these steps:

1. Identify the specific task or goal you want to work on.
2. Determine the exact time, location, and conditions under which you will complete the task.
3. Write down your implementation intention, for example: *"I will work on my project for 30 minutes at my desk immediately after breakfast."*

Habit Stacking

This technique involves attaching a new habit to an existing one, making it easier to remember and execute. By leveraging an existing habit, you can piggyback off its automaticity and integrate a new behavior seamlessly. Here's how to use habit stacking:

1. Identify a habit you already perform consistently.
2. Select a new behavior you want to incorporate into your routine.
3. Attach the new behavior immediately after the existing habit, creating a clear cue and reminder. For example, if you want to start reading more, you can stack it onto your existing habit of brushing your teeth by committing to reading for 10 minutes right after brushing.

The Pomodoro Technique

This technique involves breaking your work into intervals, typically 25 minutes of focused work followed by a short break of 5 minutes. The Pomodoro Technique helps increase productivity by providing structured and time-limited bursts of work. Here's how to implement it:

1. Choose a task you want to work on.
2. Set a timer for 25 minutes and commit to working on the task during that time.
3. When the timer goes off, take a 5-minute break to rest and recharge.
4. Repeat this cycle (called a "Pomodoro") three more times, and after the fourth Pomodoro, take a longer break of around 15 to 30 minutes.

Gamification

This technique involves incorporating game-like elements into your tasks or goals to make them more engaging and enjoyable. By adding elements such as rewards, challenges, and progress tracking, you can increase motivation and productivity. Here's how to implement gamification:

1. Define clear goals and milestones for your task or project.
2. Create a system of rewards or points that you can earn as you make progress.
3. Set up challenges or mini-games within the task to make it more interactive and stimulating.
4. Track your progress visually, using charts, graphs, or progress bars, to provide a sense of achievement and motivate further action.

Remember, these techniques may work differently for individuals, so it's important to experiment and find what works best for you.

Time-management Strategies for Overcoming Procrastination

Time management plays a crucial role in overcoming procrastination because it helps individuals prioritize tasks, set achievable goals, and allocate sufficient time for each activity. When we manage our time effectively, we can minimize distractions, avoid unnecessary delays, and maintain focus on the task at hand. This allows us to complete tasks on time, reducing the likelihood of procrastination.

Implementing time management strategies can have a significant impact on various aspects of our lives. It enables us to become more organized, reduces stress levels, and improves productivity. By effectively managing our time, we can create a sense of control over our daily activities, leading to increased motivation and a greater sense of accomplishment.

Additionally, time management helps us to find a balance between work and personal life, ensuring that we have enough time for relaxation, hobbies, and spending time with loved ones.

In Cognitive Behavioral Therapy (CBT), several time management techniques can help overcome procrastination. These techniques focus on changing our thought patterns and behaviors, leading to more efficient time management. Here are some high-level time management techniques from CBT that can be easily implemented:

1. **Prioritization**
   Start by making a to-do list and prioritize tasks based on their importance and urgency. Focus on completing high-priority tasks first to prevent them from being postponed.

2. **Break tasks into smaller steps**
   Large tasks can be overwhelming and contribute to procrastination. Break them down into smaller, manageable steps to make them more approachable and less daunting.

3. **Time blocking**

   Allocate specific time slots for different tasks or activities. This helps create structure and ensures that each task receives adequate attention. Use a planner or digital calendar to schedule your activities.

4. **Set realistic goals**

   Set specific, measurable, attainable, relevant, and time-bound (SMART) goals. Breaking down larger goals into smaller milestones can make them more achievable and reduce the tendency to procrastinate.

5. **Eliminate distractions**

   Identify and minimize distractions that hinder productivity. This may involve turning off phone notifications, creating a designated workspace, or using website blockers to limit access to distracting websites.

6. **Reward system**

   Set up a reward system to motivate yourself. After completing a task or reaching a milestone, give yourself a small reward, such as a short break, a favorite snack, or a quick walk outside.

The secret to overcoming procrastination and mastering time management lies within our ability to align our goals with our values and priorities.

As renowned productivity expert Brian Tracy once said, "*The key to success is to focus our conscious mind on things we desire, not things we fear.*" By identifying what truly matters to us and reminding ourselves of the long-term rewards that await us, we can find the inner motivation to take action and avoid falling into the trap of procrastination.

Remember, every moment wasted is an opportunity lost, but every moment seized is a step closer to achieving our dreams. Embrace the power of the present, harness your determination, and let your actions speak louder than your doubts. You have the ability to transform your relationship with time and conquer procrastination once and for all. Start now, for tomorrow is a gift waiting to be unwrapped.

Conquering Procrastination and Time Management Worksheet

Instructions: This worksheet is designed to help you overcome procrastination and improve your time management skills. It is meant to be fun and engaging, providing you with practical exercises and inspiring quotes to motivate you along the way. Remember, the key to success lies in taking action. Let's get started!

1. Reflect on Your Procrastination Habits:
- Take a few moments to list three tasks you have been consistently putting off.
- Write down how procrastinating on these tasks has affected your productivity and overall well-being.

2. Set SMART Goals:
- Choose one task from your list and set a Specific, Measurable, Achievable, Relevant, and Time-bound (SMART) goal for completing it.
- Write down your goal below, along with a deadline for completing it.

Goal: _____

Deadline: _____

3. Visualize Success:
- Close your eyes and imagine yourself completing the task successfully.
- Describe in vivid detail how you feel and the positive outcomes that result from completing the task.
- Write down your visualization experience below.

Visualization: _____

4. Break It Down:
- Break your chosen task into smaller, manageable steps.
- Write down the steps required to complete the task below.

Steps:
1. _____
2. _____
3. _____
4. _____
5. _____

5. Time Blocking:
- Select a specific time slot in your daily schedule dedicated solely to working on your chosen task.
- Write down the designated time slot below.

Time Slot: _____

6. Motivational Quotes:
- Read the following quotes and choose one that resonates with you. Write it down and refer to it whenever you need an extra boost of motivation.

a) *"The best way to get started is to quit talking and begin doing."* - Walt Disney

b) *"You don't have to be great to start, but you have to start to be great."* - Zig Ziglar

c) *"The future depends on what you do today."* - Mahatma Gandhi

d) *"Success is not final, failure is not fatal: It is the courage to continue that counts."* - Winston Churchill

Chosen Quote: _____

7. Accountability Partners:
- Find an accountability partner who will support and encourage you throughout your journey.
- Write down the name of your chosen accountability partner below.

Accountability Partner: _____

8. Celebrate Your Success:
- Once you complete your chosen task, reward yourself.
- Write down a small reward you will give yourself upon completion.

Reward: _____

Remember, this worksheet is just a starting point. Adapt it to suit your needs and keep it fun and engaging. Good luck on your journey to overcoming procrastination and mastering time management!

Chapter 9
Conquering Negative Emotions with CBT

Negative emotions such as shame, guilt, regret, jealousy, and the impact of criticism can have a profound impact on our mental well-being. They can hinder our ability to live fulfilling lives and impede our personal growth.

Cognitive Behavioral Therapy (CBT) is a powerful therapeutic approach that can help individuals navigate and conquer negative emotions. CBT focuses on identifying and challenging unhelpful thoughts and beliefs that contribute to negative emotions, ultimately leading to positive behavioral changes.

Addressing Negative Emotions

Let's talk about conquering some of the most destructive and debilitating emotions that we all experience at some point in our lives: *shame, guilt, regret, jealousy,* and *criticism*. These emotions can weigh us down, hinder our progress, and prevent us from living our lives to the fullest. But fear not because I am here to share with you the power of Cognitive Behavioral Therapy (CBT) in addressing and overcoming these negative emotions.

Let's start by understanding each of these emotions and how they can impact someone.

1. **Shame** is that overwhelming feeling of worthlessness and inadequacy. It strips away our self-esteem and leaves us feeling small and insignificant.

2. **Guilt**, on the other hand, is the nagging voice in our heads that tells us we have done something wrong, leading to self-condemnation and a sense of moral responsibility.

3. **Regret** is the bitter pill we swallow when we realize that we have missed an opportunity or made a wrong decision, causing us to dwell on the past and fill our minds with "what ifs".

4. **Jealousy** is the green-eyed monster that arises when we compare ourselves to others and covet what they have, leading to resentment and bitterness.

5. **Criticism**, whether it comes from others or our own self-talk, erodes our self-confidence and fuels self-doubt.

Now, *what makes these emotions so difficult to conquer?*

It is the power they hold over our thoughts and perceptions. They distort our thinking, making us believe that we are unworthy, that we deserve punishment, that the past cannot be changed, and that we are in constant competition with others.

These distorted thoughts become deeply ingrained in our minds, creating negative thinking patterns that are hard to break free from.

Cognitive Behavioral Therapy is a therapeutic approach that focuses on identifying and challenging these negative thoughts and beliefs and replacing them with more rational and empowering ones.

It provides us with practical techniques to change our thinking patterns and behaviors, leading to a healthier and more positive mindset.

So, *how can we apply CBT techniques in processing these emotions?* Let me share with you some advice and techniques.

Self-compassion

It is crucial to practice self-compassion. We are often our own harshest critics, but by practicing self-compassion, we can learn to treat ourselves with kindness and understanding. When shame, guilt, regret, jealousy, or criticism arise, remind yourself that you are human, that making mistakes is a part of life, and that you are worthy of love and acceptance.

Here are some ways to practice self-compassion in Cognitive Behavioral Therapy (CBT):

1. Write yourself a compassionate letter.
Take a few minutes to write a letter to yourself filled with kindness, understanding, and encouragement. Remind yourself of your worth, strengths, and progress. Read the letter whenever you need a boost of self-compassion.

Take this as a sample letter.

Dear [Your Name],

I want to take a moment to remind you of your worth, your strengths, and the progress you have made. I know that there are times when you feel overwhelmed by shame, guilt, regret, jealousy, and criticism, but I want you to know that you are so much more than those feelings.

Shame may sometimes consume you, making you feel unworthy and small. But remember, my dear, that you are deserving of love and compassion. You have made mistakes, just like everyone else, but those mistakes do not define you. You are a human being, capable of growth and change. Embrace your imperfections and learn from them, for they are a part of your beautiful journey.

Guilt is a heavy burden to carry, but it is important to remember that it serves a purpose. It shows that you have a conscience and that you care about the impact of your actions. However, dwelling in guilt for too long can be detrimental. Forgive yourself, my dear, for the mistakes you have made. Allow yourself to learn and grow from them. Use your guilt as a driving force to make amends and become a better person.

Regret can weigh heavily on your heart, constantly reminding you of missed opportunities and choices you wish you could change. But my dear, life is filled with twists and turns, and we cannot always predict the outcome. Instead of dwelling on what could have been, focus on what can be. Embrace the lessons you have learned from your regrets and use them to shape a brighter future.

Jealousy can consume you, making you feel inadequate and resentful. But remember, my dear, that comparison is the thief of joy. Your journey is unique, and so are your accomplishments. Celebrate the successes of others, knowing that your time will come. Focus on your own path, and trust that you are exactly where you need to be.

The impact of criticism can be harsh and hurtful, but let it serve as an opportunity for growth. Remember that not everyone's opinion matters. Surround yourself with those who uplift and support you. Be your own biggest cheerleader, my dear. Celebrate your victories, no matter how small, and be proud of the person you are becoming.

Above all, remember that you are worthy of love, compassion, and self-acceptance. Embrace your strengths and use them to overcome the challenges you face. You are resilient, courageous, and capable of greatness. Believe in yourself, my dear, for you are deserving of all the kindness and understanding in the world.

With love and compassion,

[Your Name]

2. Practice self-compassionate self-talk.

Pay attention to your inner dialogue and replace self-critical thoughts with compassionate and understanding ones. Instead of berating yourself for making a mistake, offer yourself understanding and support, just as you would a close friend.

Sample self-compassionate self-talk:

"I made a mistake today, and that's okay. Everyone makes mistakes; it's a part of being human. I understand that I was trying my best in that situation, and sometimes things just don't go as planned. It's important for me to be kind to myself and learn from this experience instead of beating myself up over it. I will use this as an opportunity to grow and improve, and I will remember to be patient and forgiving with myself along the way. I deserve compassion and understanding, just like anyone else."

3. Develop a self-compassion mantra.

Create a short, positive phrase that encapsulates self-compassion for you. Repeat this mantra whenever you need a reminder to be kind and understanding towards yourself.

Here are some you can use:

"I am deserving of love and kindness, especially from myself."
"I embrace my imperfections and treat myself with gentle understanding."
"I am enough, just as I am, and I deserve compassion."
"I forgive myself for my mistakes and choose to learn and grow from them."

"I am my own best friend, offering myself compassion in times of need."

"I give myself permission to prioritize self-care and nourish my well-being."

"I release self-judgment and embrace self-compassion in every moment."

"I honor my emotions and grant myself the space to heal and grow."

"I am worthy of kindness, understanding, and unconditional love."

"I choose to be gentle with myself, knowing that I am doing the best I can."

4. Engage in self-care activities.

Prioritize activities that nurture and nourish you. This could include activities such as taking a warm bath, going for a walk in nature, reading a book, or practicing mindfulness. Engaging in self-care regularly is an act of self-compassion.

Here are some unique and powerful self-care activities that you can consider:

- **Forest bathing:** Take a trip to a nearby forest or park and immerse yourself in nature. Allow yourself to connect with the trees, breathe in the fresh air, and let the serenity of the surroundings calm your mind.

- **Sound therapy:** Explore the healing power of sound by listening to soothing music, using singing bowls, or trying a sound meditation. The vibrations and tones can help relax your body, reduce stress, and promote overall well-being.

- **Art therapy:** Engage in a creative activity like painting, drawing, or sculpting. Allow yourself to express your emotions and thoughts through art, which can be therapeutic and provide a sense of release and self-discovery.

- **Digital detox:** Disconnect from technology for a day or even just a few hours. Put your phone on silent, turn off notifications, and take a break from screens. Use this time to focus on activities that don't involve technology, such as journaling, going for a hike, or spending quality time with loved ones.

- **Dance therapy:** Put on your favorite music and let your body move freely. Dancing can be a fun and liberating way to release tension, boost your mood, and increase your energy levels.

- **Volunteering:** Give back to your community by engaging in volunteer work. Find a cause or organization that resonates with you and dedicate some time to making a positive impact. Helping others can give you a sense of fulfillment and purpose.

- **Mindful eating:** Take the time to savor your meals and eat mindfully. Pay attention to the flavors, textures, and sensations of the food. Practice gratitude for nourishing your body and try to eat without distractions.

- **Float therapy:** Experience the weightlessness and relaxation of floating in a sensory deprivation tank. This therapy involves floating in a tank filled with warm salt water, providing deep relaxation and stress relief.

Remember, self-care is about finding activities that resonate with you and bring you joy, relaxation, and rejuvenation. Experiment with different activities and find what works best for you.

5. Practice self-compassionate forgiveness.
Reflect on any self-blame or guilt you may be carrying and consciously choose to forgive yourself. Recognize that making mistakes is part of being human and that you deserve forgiveness, just like anyone else.

6. Engage in self-affirmations.
Create a list of positive affirmations that reflect your self-worth and repeat them to yourself daily. Affirmations such as *"I am worthy of love and compassion"* or *"I deserve kindness and understanding"* can help cultivate self-compassion.

> *I am worthy of love and forgiveness, and I release any shame or guilt that weighs me down. I acknowledge my past mistakes, but I choose to learn from them and grow into a better version of myself.*

> *I let go of regret and embrace the opportunities for growth that lie ahead. I trust in the journey of life, knowing that every experience has shaped me into who I am today.*

I acknowledge that jealousy is a natural emotion, but I choose not to let it consume me. I celebrate the successes and happiness of others, knowing that their achievements do not diminish my own worth.

=I release the need to criticize myself or others. I choose to focus on compassion, understanding, and supporting those around me. I believe in the power of kindness and uplifting words.

=I am imperfect, but I am also resilient and capable of change. I choose to forgive myself and others, knowing that we are all human and prone to mistakes. I embrace my growth and celebrate the journey of self-improvement.

=I am worthy of love, forgiveness, and happiness. I choose to let go of shame, guilt, regret, jealousy, and criticism and embrace a life filled with self-acceptance, compassion, and personal growth.

7. Seek support from others.

Reach out to trusted friends, family, or a therapist to discuss your struggles and receive support. Sharing your experiences and feelings with others can help you feel validated and receive compassion from those around you.

Remember, self-compassion is a skill that takes practice and patience. Be gentle with yourself as you explore these techniques and find what works best for you.

Challenging Your Thoughts and Beliefs

When these negative emotions arise, question the validity of the thoughts that accompany them. Are they based on facts or distorted perceptions? Are you jumping to conclusions or catastrophizing? By challenging these thoughts, you can start to break free from their grip and replace them with more rational and empowering ones.

In Cognitive Behavioral Therapy (CBT), challenging and changing negative thoughts is a key component to addressing emotions such as shame, guilt, regret, jealousy, and criticism. Here are some steps to challenge your thoughts during these emotions:

1. **Identify the negative thought:** Start by becoming aware of the specific negative thought that is contributing to your emotion. For example, if you're feeling guilty, the thought might be, *"I should have done better."*

2. **Evaluate the evidence:** Examine the evidence for and against the negative thought. Ask yourself if there are any facts or evidence that support or contradict the thought. For instance, if you feel guilty about not completing a task, consider whether there were any valid reasons or circumstances that hindered you.

3. **Consider alternative explanations:** Generate alternative explanations or interpretations for the situation. Ask yourself if there could be any other valid perspectives or reasons for your actions. This can help you challenge the automatic negative thoughts that tend to arise during these emotions.

4. **Examine the consequences:** Reflect on the consequences of holding onto the negative thought. Consider how it affects your emotions, behaviors, and overall well-being. Recognize that dwelling on these thoughts may not be helpful or productive.

5. **Challenge cognitive distortions:** Identify and challenge cognitive distortions, which are common thinking errors that contribute to negative emotions. Examples include all-or-nothing thinking, overgeneralization, and jumping to conclusions. Replace these distortions with more balanced and realistic thoughts.

6. **Seek evidence from others:** Consider seeking input or feedback from trusted friends, family, or professionals who can provide an objective viewpoint. They may offer alternative perspectives or help challenge your negative thoughts.

7. **Practice self-compassion:** Remind yourself that everyone makes mistakes and experiences negative emotions. Treat yourself with kindness and understanding, just as you would a friend in a similar situation. Practice self-compassion to counteract feelings of shame, guilt, regret, jealousy, or criticism.

8. **Replace with positive thoughts:** Once you have challenged and evaluated the negative thoughts, replace them with positive and affirming thoughts. For example, if you feel jealous of someone's success, remind yourself of your own accomplishments and strengths.

Remember, challenging negative thoughts takes practice and patience. It is a skill that can be developed over time with consistent effort and self-reflection.

Practice Gratitude

I encourage you to practice gratitude. Gratitude is a powerful antidote to jealousy and resentment. Take a moment each day to reflect on the things you are grateful for, no matter how small. This practice shifts your focus from what you don't have to what you do have, cultivating a sense of contentment and appreciation.

> **Gratitude Exercise: Overcoming Negative Emotions**
> Instructions:
>
> 1. Find a quiet and comfortable space where you can sit or lie down without distractions.
> 2. Close your eyes and take a few deep breaths, allowing yourself to relax and let go of any tension in your body.
> 3. Reflect on the negative emotions you want to overcome, such as shame, regret, guilt, jealousy, or criticism. Allow yourself to fully acknowledge and feel these emotions without judgment.
> 4. Now, shift your focus to gratitude. Begin by thinking of three things you are grateful for in your life right now. They can be simple things like having a roof over your head, good health, or the support of loved ones.

5. As you think of each thing you are grateful for, try to visualize it in your mind and feel the positive emotions associated with it. Imagine how it enhances your life and brings you joy.
6. Take a moment to fully immerse yourself in the feelings of gratitude and appreciation. Allow these emotions to fill your entire being.
7. Now, think of three positive qualities or strengths that you possess. It could be something like kindness, creativity, or resilience. Reflect on how these qualities have benefited you and others.
8. Once again, visualize each quality or strength and feel the positive emotions that arise from recognizing them. Embrace the sense of self-worth and pride that comes with acknowledging your own positive attributes.
9. Take a few more deep breaths, allowing the gratitude and positive emotions to sink in and replace the negative emotions you were experiencing earlier.
10. When you feel ready, slowly open your eyes and bring your attention back to the present moment.

Repeat this exercise whenever you find yourself overwhelmed by negative emotions. Regular practice can help shift your mindset towards gratitude and cultivate a more positive outlook on life.

Reframing

Another technique to conquer these emotions is reframing. Reframing involves looking at a situation from a different perspective. When guilt or regret arises, ask yourself, *"What can I learn from this experience?"* or *"How can I grow from this?"* By reframing these emotions as opportunities for growth and learning, you can transform them into catalysts for personal development.

One creative way to do reframing in Cognitive Behavioral Therapy (CBT) to overcome shame, guilt, regret, jealousy, and criticism is through the use of a *"Self-Compassion Gallery."*

Step 1: Setting up the Gallery
1. Find a quiet and comfortable space where you can create your Self-Compassion Gallery. This can be a physical space or a virtual one, such as a digital vision board or slideshow.
2. Gather materials such as magazines, photographs, art supplies, or digital images that represent self-compassion, positivity, and personal growth.

Step 2: Identify Negative Thoughts and Emotions
1. Begin by identifying the negative thoughts and emotions associated with shame, guilt, regret, jealousy, and criticism. Write them down or create a mental list.
2. For each negative thought or emotion, identify a specific event or situation where it occurred. Write down a brief description of each event.

Step 3: Reframing and Creating Artifacts

1. Take one negative thought or emotion at a time and reframe it in a more compassionate and positive light. For example, if the negative thought is *"I feel guilty for not spending enough time with my family,"* reframe it as *"I acknowledge that I am doing my best, and I prioritize quality time when I can."*
2. Create artifacts for each reframed thought or emotion using the materials you gathered. For physical spaces, you can create collages, drawings, or paintings. For virtual spaces, use digital images, quotes, or even short videos that represent the reframed thoughts and emotions.
3. Get creative and make each artifact visually appealing and personally meaningful. Add colors, words, symbols, or any elements that resonate with you and evoke self-compassion.

Step 4: Assemble Your Self-Compassion Gallery

1. Arrange the artifacts in your chosen space, either physically or digitally. You can create a chronological order or arrange them randomly, whatever feels right for you.
2. Take a moment to step back and observe your gallery. Reflect on the positive reframes and the compassionate messages conveyed by each artifact.
3. Whenever negative thoughts or emotions arise, visit your Self-Compassion Gallery and focus on the corresponding reframed thoughts and emotions. Allow yourself to be immersed in self-compassion and positivity.

Step 5: Regular Reflection and Reinforcement
1. Set aside regular time to reflect on your Self-Compassion Gallery. This may be daily, weekly, or whenever you feel the need for self-compassion reinforcement.
2. During reflection, revisit the artifacts and their reframed thoughts and emotions. Internalize these messages and remind yourself of the progress you've made in reframing negative thoughts and emotions.
3. Use this reflection time to reinforce self-compassion and challenge any lingering shame, guilt, regret, jealousy, or criticism.
4. Over time, as you continue to engage with your Self-Compassion Gallery, notice how your perspective shifts and how you become more resilient to negative thoughts and emotions.

Remember, the Self-Compassion Gallery is a personal and creative tool to support your journey toward overcoming negative thoughts and emotions. Tailor it to your own preferences, and always seek professional guidance if needed.

Lastly, surround yourself with positive and supportive people. Seek out those who uplift you, who celebrate your successes, and who remind you of your inherent worth. Build a network of individuals who believe in you and encourage you to be your best self. Their support and encouragement will empower you to conquer these negative emotions and live a life of fulfillment and joy. May you find the strength to conquer these emotions and live a life of fulfillment.

Conclusion

The key message of CBT is that we have the power to change our thoughts and behaviors, which, in turn, can positively influence our emotions and overall mental health. It emphasizes the importance of taking an active role in managing our thoughts and behaviors to improve our quality of life.

As you reach the end of this CBT guide, take a moment to reflect on the key concepts and techniques you have learned. Remember, seeking professional help is crucial when needed, as they can provide guidance and support tailored to your specific needs.

32 CBT Techniques for a Better Life

Depression	
Identifying Negative Thinking Patterns	Recognizing and challenging negative thoughts that contribute to depression.
Positive Affirmations, Self-compassion, and Mindfulness	Fostering positive self-talk, self-acceptance, and present moment awareness to alleviate depression.
Behavioral Activation Techniques	Engaging in activities that bring pleasure and a sense of accomplishment to combat depression.

Anxiety	
Cognitive Restructuring for Anxiety	Identifying and challenging irrational thoughts that contribute to anxiety.
Relaxation and Stress Management Techniques	Utilizing relaxation exercises to reduce anxiety and manage stress effectively.
Exposure Therapy and Desensitization Techniques	Gradual exposure to anxiety-provoking situations to overcome fears and phobias.
OCD	
Practicing Cognitive Flexibility	Developing the ability to adapt and change rigid thought patterns associated with OCD.
Using Anxiety Reduction Methods	Employing techniques to reduce anxiety levels experienced in OCD.
Exposure and Response Prevention (ERP) Techniques for OCD	Gradually facing and resisting compulsive behaviors to reduce OCD symptoms.
Addiction	
Identifying and Challenging Automatic Thoughts	Recognizing and challenging automatic thoughts that contribute to addictive behaviors.

Identifying Triggers and High-risk Situations	Identifying situations or cues that may lead to relapse and developing strategies to avoid them.
Coping Skills to Prevent Relapse	Equipping individuals with effective coping mechanisms to prevent relapse in addiction.
Insomnia	
Sleep Education	Providing knowledge and understanding about sleep to improve insomnia management.
Cognitive Restructuring for Sleep-related Thoughts	Addressing and modifying negative thoughts and beliefs about sleep to promote better sleep
Sleep Hygiene	Establishing healthy habits and routines to improve sleep quality.
Relaxation and Mindfulness Techniques for Better Sleep	Using relaxation and mindfulness exercises to promote relaxation and improve sleep.
Establishing Bed-Sleep Association for Better Sleep Quality	Associating the bed with sleep to enhance sleep quality and reduce insomnia.

Enhancing Sleep Efficiency through Sleep Restriction	Restricting time in bed to increase sleep efficiency and reduce time spent awake in bed.
Sustaining Healthy Sleep Patterns with Maintenance Strategies	Developing strategies to maintain healthy sleep patterns and prevent relapse into insomnia.
Stress	
Identifying Stress Triggers in CBT	Identifying situations or factors that cause stress and developing strategies to manage them.
Challenging Stress-inducing Thoughts	Questioning and reframing negative thoughts that contribute to stress.
Relaxation Techniques to Reduce Stress	Utilizing relaxation exercises to promote relaxation and reduce stress levels.
Thought Stopping Technique for Stress Management	Interrupting and replacing anxious or stressful thoughts with more positive ones.
Behavioral Activation for Stress	Engaging in enjoyable and fulfilling activities to counteract the effects of stress.
Procrastination	
Cognitive Restructuring to Overcome Procrastination	Identifying and challenging thoughts and beliefs that contribute to procrastination.

Behavioral Techniques to Increase Motivation and Productivity	Implementing strategies to enhance motivation and productivity levels.
Time-management Strategies for Overcoming Procrastination	Developing techniques to manage time effectively and overcome procrastination.
Conquer Procrastination and Master Time Management	Combining cognitive and behavioral strategies to overcome procrastination and improve time management.
Shame, Guilt, Regret, Jealousy, and Criticism	
Self-compassion	Cultivating kindness and understanding towards oneself to overcome negative emotions.
Challenging Your Thoughts and Beliefs	Questioning and reframing negative thoughts and beliefs that contribute to negative emotions.
Practice Gratitude	Cultivating a sense of appreciation and focusing on positive aspects of life to overcome negative emotions.
Reframing	Viewing situations from a different perspective to change negative emotions into positive ones.

Now, it's time to take what you've learned and implement these CBT strategies in your life. Embrace the power of CBT and witness its transformative effects on your mental health and overall well-being.

This is where the real work begins.

Implementing CBT strategies may come with its own set of challenges, but remember that you have the power to overcome them. Building resilience is key in this process. It involves developing the ability to bounce back from setbacks and face difficulties head-on.

Cultivating positive habits, such as practicing self-care and challenging negative thoughts, will help reinforce your progress. Remember, motivation may fluctuate, but with commitment and perseverance, you can maintain your momentum.

Trust the process and believe in yourself, for this journey is about transforming your mind and finding inner peace.

Your journey towards a fulfilling life starts now.

Thank you, and may your journey be filled with love, growth, and lasting transformation.

> *"Yesterday, I was clever, so I wanted to change the world. Today I am wise, so I am changing myself."* - **Rumi**

References

Beck, J. S. (2011). Cognitive behavior therapy: Basics and beyond. Guilford Press.

Clark, D. A., & Beck, A. T. (2010). Cognitive therapy of anxiety disorders: Science and practice. Guilford Press.

Dobson, K. S., & Dobson, D. (2018). Evidence-based practice of cognitive-behavioral therapy. Guilford Publications.

Emmelkamp, P. M., & Ehring, T. (2018). The Wiley handbook of cognitive behavioral therapy. John Wiley & Sons.

Leahy, R. L. (2017). Cognitive therapy techniques: A practitioner's guide. Guilford Publications.

Neenan, M., & Dryden, W. (2014). Cognitive therapy: 100 key points and techniques. Routledge.

Padesky, C. A., & Greenberger, D. (1995). Clinician's guide to Mind Over Mood. Guilford Press.

Persons, J. B. (2008). The case formulation approach to cognitive-behavior therapy. Guilford Press.

Roth, A., & Fonagy, P. (2013). What works for whom?: A critical review of psychotherapy research. Guilford Press.

Segal, Z. V., Williams, J. M., & Teasdale, J. D. (2013). Mindfulness-based cognitive therapy for depression. Guilford Press.

Wells, A. (2011). Metacognitive therapy for anxiety and depression. Guilford Press.

American Psychological Association. (2017). Understanding Cognitive Behavioral Therapy. Retrieved from https://www.apa.org/ptsd-guideline/treatments/cognitive-behavioral-therapy.pdf

Beck Institute for Cognitive Behavior Therapy. (n.d.). What is Cognitive Therapy? Retrieved from https://beckinstitute.org/get-informed/what-is-cognitive-therapy/

British Association for Behavioural and Cognitive Psychotherapies. (n.d.). What is CBT? Retrieved from https://www.babcp.com/files/About/CBT-Today/What-is-CBT.pdf

Canadian Psychological Association. (2020). Fact Sheet: Cognitive-Behavioral Therapy. Retrieved from https://cpa.ca/psychologyfactsheets/cognitive-behavioral-therapy/

Centre for Clinical Interventions. (2017). Cognitive-Behavioural Therapy. Retrieved from https://www.cci.health.wa.gov.au/Resources/Looking-After-Yourself/Cognitive-Behavioural-Therapy

Mayo Clinic. (2020). Cognitive Behavioral Therapy. Retrieved from https://www.mayoclinic.org/tests-procedures/cognitive-behavioral-therapy/about/pac-20384610

National Institute of Mental Health. (2016). Psychotherapies. Retrieved from https://www.nimh.nih.gov/health/topics/psychotherapies/index.shtml

National Health Service. (2019). Cognitive Behavioural Therapy (CBT). Retrieved from https://www.nhs.uk/conditions/cognitive-behavioural-therapy-cbt/

Psychology Today. (2020). Cognitive Behavioral Therapy (CBT). Retrieved from https://www.psychologytoday.com/us/therapy-types/cognitive-behavioral-therapy

Substance Abuse and Mental Health Services Administration. (2015). Treatment for Substance Use Disorders. Retrieved from https://store.samhsa.gov/product/Treatment-for-Substance-Use-Disorders/SMA15-4006

World Health Organization. (2019). Mental health. Retrieved from https://www.who.int/mental_health/management/en/

University of Oxford. (n.d.). Cognitive Behavioral Therapy (CBT). Retrieved from https://www.psych.ox.ac.uk/research/cognitive-behavioural-therapy

University of California, Berkeley. (n.d.). Cognitive-Behavioral Therapy (CBT). Retrieved from https://uhs.berkeley.edu/counseling/therapy

Harvard Medical School. (2019). Cognitive Behavioral Therapy. Retrieved from https://www.health.harvard.edu/blog/cognitive-behavioral-therapy-could-work-better-for-insomnia-than-drugs-or-herbal-remedies-201209145103

Yale School of Medicine. (n.d.). Cognitive Behavioral Therapy (CBT). Retrieved from https://medicine.yale.edu/psychiatry/education/medstudents/curriculum/psycknowledge/cbt.aspx

Exclusive Bonuses

Dear Readers,

A CBT journey is a transformative experience that empowers you to take control of your thoughts and behaviors, leading to positive changes in your mental health and well-being. Accompanying this book on CBT are FREE exclusive resources that aim to enhance your journey toward well-being and self-discovery.

1. **Healing Affirmation Cards:** Featuring daily affirmations and corresponding exercises to uplift and guide you. The Healing Affirmation Cards are designed to infuse positivity and motivation into your daily routine, encouraging self-reflection and growth through powerful affirmations and exercises. Unlock a treasure trove of inspiration and healing energy that will complement your CBT practice.

2. **Self-care Tool Kit:** Filled with resources for healing and renewal. The Self-care Tool Kit serves as a valuable resource to support your well-being journey, providing practical tools and exercises to nurture yourself and promote self-love. Claim this bonus to access a comprehensive collection of self-care resources that will empower you in your healing and growth journey.

3. **Practical Guide to DBT:** Designed to provide you with a clear and practical understanding of Dialectical Behavior Therapy. The Practical Guide to DBT offers an introduction to Dialectical Behavior Therapy, guiding you through the core principles and techniques of this transformative approach.

4. **Guide to Practicing ACT:** Offers insights into the transformative power of Acceptance Commitment Therapy. The Guide to Practicing ACT introduces you to the transformative magic of Acceptance Commitment Therapy, offering practical tips and exercises to help you effectively practice ACT in your daily life.

How to Access Your Bonuses:
Simply use your smartphone to scan the QR Code below, and you will be directed to the bonus content.

These exclusive bonuses as tools to enhance your CBT journey. May these resources inspire and empower you to embrace healing, self-discovery, and growth as you navigate the path to well-being. Thank you for sharing with me your journey toward mental wellness and self-improvement. Wishing you strength and resilience throughout this transformative experience.

Warm regards,

Charles Kerwood